DREAM SEEDS

by
Mike Murdock

Wisdom is the principal thing; therefore get wisdom:
and with all thy getting get understanding.
Proverbs 4:7

Wisdom Training Center
P.O. Box 99
Dallas, Texas 75221

Unless otherwise indicated, all Scripture quotations
are taken from the *King James Version* of the Bible.

Dream Seeds
ISBN 0-89274-392-1
Copyright by Mike Murdock
P.O. Box 99
Dallas, Texas 75221

Published by
Wisdom International
P.O. Box 747
Dallas, Texas 75221

Contents

Acknowledgments

My deep gratitude to my dedicated, loyal and efficient staff who doubled up on their duties to enable me to finish this book: Jena Taylor, Tammie Smith, Gail Davis, Mike Hodge, Brenda Hodge, Jackie Horan, Penny Harding, Karen Adlong, John Murdock III, and Diana Windmiller.

My very special thanks to my dear friend Joanne Derstine whose editorial assistance and constant motivation kept me going in the wee hours of the morning until we completed this manuscript.

To my faith partners whose prayers and support continue to make my own Dream Seed to "mend broken people" come true.

Searching for the Keys

Dream Seeds

I WALKED OUT OF THE COURTROOM, my mind in a daze.

With one stroke of his pen, the judge had stripped me of nearly everything I possessed, everything that had been dear to me.

My 13-year marriage had crumbled, my house and furnishings swept away, my finances totally depleted. I was drowning in a sea of attorney's fees and unpaid bills.

DEVASTATED

My world, once storybook perfect and the image of the energetic young evangelist with supportive, loving family, had been crushed by the unthinkable, the unpardonable. *I was alone.*

That ugly afternoon as I stood on the steps of the courthouse, I felt drained and confused. My mind cried out, *What in the world went wrong?* I really could not point my finger at anyone.

Feverishly, I clawed my way through the debris of my memory and could not understand how this had happened to me. *Not me.*

"Lord, I've preached miracles, prosperity and how your blessings are for us today – and here I stand stripped and humiliated before man and Heaven. My bank account is exhausted. The credibility of my ministry is in jeopardy. The deepest love I have ever known has been ripped to shreds. Is this what I have to show for your blessings upon my life?"

1

In the midst of my confusion, suddenly there came to me the calmest voice I'd ever heard:

"I'm not through blessing you."

Somehow, I believed those words God spoke to me that day. In fact, it was then that I wrote the song, "God's Not Through Blessing You."

God's Not Through Blessing You

"A man one day lost every dime
    to his name.
His best friends even said he
    was through.
But God said to Job, 'Your best
    days are just ahead,
'Cause I'm not through blessing
    you.'

"God's not through blessing
    you,
God's not through blessing you.
So never give up, what He said
    He will do,
God's not through blessing
    you."

At that moment, I knew God would find a way to restore His blessings upon my life.

"And I will restore to you the years that the locust hath eaten, the cankerworm, and the caterpillar, and the palmerworm..." (Joel 2:25).

I DETERMINED TO FIND THOSE KEYS THAT WOULD UNLOCK THE WINDOWS OF HEAVEN.

My search began immediately. It was a grueling process. A maelstrom of emotions churned within me. Loneliness stalked me relentlessly. I found myself bursting into tears at unexpected times. My memory became my enemy as I constantly replayed the past.

After listening to me pray and cry for three hours one day, God simply spoke two words, *"Shut up!"*

I suddenly realized that I should *stop* concentrating on what I had *lost* and begin *focusing* on what I *still possessed*. Within hours He gave me two songs - "You Can Make It" and "I Am Blessed." (He has used these songs to bless countless thousands since that day. For that, I give Him the glory.)

Gradually the light began to dawn.

Those sought-after laws of blessing began to surface. My emotions began to settle. The pain subsided.

I began to dream again.

I awakened one morning with new energy, fresh ideas and the greatest anointing I had ever known. Yes, even a river of financial blessing began to flow back into my life.

Most thrilling of all, God revealed to me the Master Keys that unlocked these miracles.

Your life may be difficult for you right now. You may be searching frantically for a solution to a family crisis. Perhaps your weekly paycheck just doesn't stretch sufficiently to pay your bills. You may be in desperate need of a healing in your body. You may feel like a failure.

You may feel as though you don't even deserve a miracle.

Well, my friend, *I wrote this book for you!* Whatever problem you are facing, I know these MASTER KEYS TO MIRACLES AND BLESSINGS will work for you as they did for me. Feel free to underline any thought that helps you. Keep this book handy. Review it often. I believe you are on the threshold of the greatest miracles you've ever experienced in your entire life!

What is the greatest miracle God could do for you today?

What do you dream of doing with your life? What blessing are you pursuing? *What would you attempt to do if you knew it was impossible to fail?* What dream dominates you?

It may *appear unattainable*, it may seem impossible, *yet the picture persists within you.*

There is a reason.

You see, God *begins* every miracle in your life with a *seed-picture* – the invisible idea that gives birth to a visible blessing.

Our dreams and desires begin as *photographs* within our hearts and minds – things we want to happen in our future. God plants these pictures as *invisible seeds* within us.

I call these invisible photographs of desired miracles and blessings DREAM SEEDS. Dream Seeds are the invisible visions within you planted by God – not a carnal creation of an unholy imagination.

So the first thing to do is make sure that what you think is a DREAM SEED is in line with God's will and Word and is from Him.

Miracles are not Accidents

If God loves me so much, why am I still sick? If God is so concerned about me, why doesn't He give me more money? Why am I missing out on the miracles and blessings that others seem to be enjoying?

These thoughts haunted me.

My father is a minister. I have four sisters and two brothers, and all of us have been raised in church. From an early age I was taught that God was a God of miracles and blessings.

But something was wrong. They just did not seem to happen very often for me.

Oh, I knew that God loved me. But the miracles promised in the Bible simply were not happening in my life.

I was determined to know the reason and began to search for the keys that made miracles happen.

My persistence paid off. I made some powerful discoveries.

These discoveries contradicted some popular teaching, and sometimes it was even *painful* for me. As you know, change is usually uncomfortable – and especially for this Irish lad!

I found that I had to learn the difference between the LOVE of God and the BLESSINGS of God.

7

His *love* is *unconditional*, but His *blessings* are *conditional*. He *loves* me because of *who I am*, but He *blesses* me because of *what I do*.

His LOVE for me is sovereign, unearned and not dependent on whether I am obedient or not.

"For God so loved the world, that He gave His only begotten Son, that whosoever believeth in Him should not perish, but have everlasting life" (John 3:16).

"But God commendeth his love toward us, in that, while we were yet sinners, Christ died for us" (Romans 5:8).

I did not initiate His love for me. But I do initiate His miracles for me. *Yes, I am the one who CHOOSES the MIRACLES that happen in my life.*

"If ye be willing and obedient, ye shall eat the good of the land." (Isaiah 1:19).

"And it shall come to pass, if thou shalt hearken diligently unto the voice of the Lord thy God, to observe and to do all his commandments which I command thee this day, that the LORD thy God will set thee on high above all nations of the earth: And all these blessings shall come on thee, and overtake thee, if thou shalt hearken unto the voice of the LORD thy God" (Deuteronomy 28:1,2).

WHAT DOES THIS REALLY MEAN?

Miracles are NOT accidents. They are NOT determined by fate or chance. They are NOT the uncontrollable actions of an unpredictable God. Rather, you and I are the ones who release

His power to make miracles happen! You and I make the decisions that create our circumstances.

Do you realize how incredible this is? God gives me the power to *participate* in the progress of my life. God gives me the *option* to succeed. He wants me to *feel* and *see* my progress. And, He wants to REWARD me for that progress.

I AM HIS CHILD. The seed of His nature is within me.

"Whereby are given unto us exceeding great and precious promises: That by these ye might be partakers of the divine nature..." (2 Peter 1:4).

I am not a robot. I am not a puppet. I am a child of God created in His image, with the *ability to believe, decide and choose* the miracles that happen in my life.

This revelation stunned me. It burst through the clouds of my life like a million suns. The Bible suddenly became my personal treasure chest. I realized it was a biography of champions who chose to be in Heaven's hall of fame. These champions were driven by a DREAM SEED deep within their spirits. Their DREAM SEED transformed them from mediocre men to men of miracles.

ABRAHAM'S DREAM SEED

Abraham had an *invisible photograph* of his many generations of children.

"Who against hope believed in hope, that he might become the father of many nations...He staggered not at the promise of God through unbelief; but was strong in faith, giving glory to God" (Romans 4:18-20).

DREAM SEED FOR HER HEALING

The hemorrhaging woman who fought the crowd to get to Jesus carried an *invisible picture* of her healing within her heart.

"For she said, if I may touch but his clothes, I shall be whole. And straightway the fountain of her blood was dried up; and she felt in her body that she was healed of that plague" (Mark 5:28,29)

Yes, God wants to bless us. He wants to do the impossible in our lives. And, He *begins* every great miracle and blessing with *an invisible photograph of the desired miracle and blessing –* your DREAM SEED.

GOD WANTS YOU HEALED AND HEALTHY

Any reputable manufacturer is committed to the success of his product. Our Heavenly Father is no exception.

"Jesus went about all the cities and villages, teaching in their synagogues, and preaching the gospel of the kingdom, and healing every sickness and every disease among the people" (Matthew 9:35).

"who healeth all thy diseases" (Psalm 103:3).

"Beloved, I wish above all things that thou mayest prosper and be in health, even as thy soul prospereth" (3 John 2).

Sickness is a *time-stealer*. Precious hours that could be spent in the work of God, ministering to your family or working on the job are forever lost.

Sickness promotes *selfishness*. It makes people focus on themselves and their own needs. It enslaves the members of their families to wait on them and pamper them in their sickness.

Sickness is a *money-waster.* Medical bills rob us of vacations, college opportunities and much-needed finances to support evangelism.

Jesus HATED sickness and disease. He saw Satan as the instigator.

"who went about doing good, and healing all that were oppressed of the devil; for God was with Him" (Acts 10:38).

In the words of the theme song I wrote for Oral Roberts' ministry, "God wants you healed, and so do I! God wants you well, whole and fully alive. And so today, whatever you need, release your faith and plant your seed. Believe! God wants you healed – and so do I!"

I'LL NEVER FORGET THE LADY IN LOUISIANA

I was about 24-years-old at the time. Before me in the prayer line stood a lady who was in pain.

Looking intently into her eyes, I asked, "Do you really believe God is going to heal you tonight?"

"Well, I really don't know," she replied. "I believe God is using this sickness to teach me something."

I vainly attempted to convince her of God's desire to heal. But she became more insistent that God was using sickness to teach her some lesson.

Exasperated, I finally asked, "Are you taking any medication?"

"Oh, yes," was her quick reply.

"Naughty, naughty," I chided. "If you believe God *wants* you to be sick, why are you sneaking behind His back trying to get well?"

Multitudes are sick today because of erroneous teaching and religious upbringing prejudiced *against* miracles. While we surely can learn from an unpleasant experience in our lives, the *Holy Spirit* is our Teacher – NOT disease.

GOD WANTS YOU CLEAN AND FORGIVEN

When we come to Him in true repentance, God cleanses us of sin and makes us pure and holy in His sight.

"As far as the east is from the west, so far hath he removed our transgressions from us" (Psalm 103:12).

GOD WANTS TO MEET YOUR FINANCIAL NEEDS

Jesus not only ministered to the sick; He also had a deep concern for the poor.

He didn't want us to *worry* about money.

"Wherefore, if God so clothe the grass of the field, which to day is, and tomorrow is cast into the oven, shall he not much more clothe you, O ye of little faith?" (Matthew 6:30).

Yes, God wants to prosper you in everything you do.

"Beloved, I wish above all things that thou mayest prosper and be in health, even as thy soul prospereth" (3 John 2).

What is prosperity? PROSPERITY IS HAVING ENOUGH OF GOD'S SUPPLY TO DO GOD'S WILL.

"But my God shall supply all your need according to his riches in glory by Christ Jesus" (Philippians 4:19).

"Who satisfieth thy mouth with good things..." (Psalm 103:5).

GOD IS YOUR SOURCE

Oral Roberts has faithfully reminded us of this truth. God may use many different methods, but *He* is the *Source* of all good things.

"Every good gift and every perfect gift is from above, and cometh down from the Father of lights, with whom is no variableness, neither shadow of turning" (James 1:17).

"But thou shalt remember the LORD thy God: for it is he that giveth thee power to get wealth..." (Deuteronomy 8:18).

SO WHAT MAKES MIRACLES AND BLESSINGS HAPPEN?

Is there a *formula* for miracles and blessings? Absolutely.

Miracles are not haphazard experiences doled out by a moody, temperamental God. Neither can they be begged or bought. *Miracles and blessings are His rewards for using our faith in Him.*

Yes, GOD WANTS TO BLESS HIS CHILDREN WITH EVERY GOOD AND PERFECT GIFT.

Now, let's reach for the first Master Key that will unlock the BIGGEST DREAM SEED you have in your life today.

13

PART **2** DREAM SEEDS

The 7 Master Keys to Miracles and Blessings

The Master Key of
RESPECT

Principle: What you respect, you will attract.

The Master Key of Respect

Remember, your DREAM SEED is the *invisible photograph within you of the desired miracle or blessing you want from God.* It may be good health, a special miracle of healing, a restored marriage, a mate, a rewarding job or whatever. *But it must be something you RESPECT enough to pursue.*

The first Master Key that I have discovered in unlocking your DREAM SEED is the key of RESPECT for your DREAM SEED.

WHAT YOU RESPECT, YOU WILL ATTRACT.

Do you want *friends*? Then begin showing respect for people. Do you desire *good health*? You must begin respecting your body. Then, establish the habits that reflect your respect for your body. Do you want *money* to flow into your life? Then use wisely what God has already given you.

Jesus taught that those who respected and appreciated what they were given would receive even more.

"Well done, thou good and faithful servant: thou hast been faithful over a few things, I will make thee ruler over many things: enter thou into the joy of thy lord" (Matthew 25:21).

You must respect what you want to come toward you.

What you don't really appreciate, you will eventually lose. It may be your teenage son, your health or your job. When you don't respect a family member, he will probably withdraw from you. When you lack respect for your body, your health deteriorates. When you become careless toward your job, you risk losing it.

WHY A GOOD MAN WAS FIRED

This reminds me of a young man who once worked for me. I liked him immensely and really felt he would always be a part of my ministry. He loved to laugh and truly seemed to enjoy his responsibilities.

But after some months, his work became sloppy. It became obvious that he didn't take my deadlines seriously. He became too comfortable with his position.

One day when his parents were visiting town, he took the liberty of leaving the office at midday, taking the remainder of the day off to be with his parents. He did the same thing the next day – both times without the consent of his supervisor.

My office manager called me long distance. "What should I do?" she asked, frustrated.

"Well, it is evident he doesn't really take his job seriously," I replied. "So let him go if you feel that it is necessary."

We hated to fire him, but his lack of caring would eventually affect the morale of our entire office and ministry. *What this young man failed to respect, he lost.*

DO YOU TRULY RESPECT YOUR DREAM SEED?

What you respect will inevitably come toward you.

Favor.

Finances.

Friends.

Zaccheus of the New Testament is an example. His respect for Christ motivated him to climb a tree just to catch a glimpse of Jesus. It was that respect and love which then motivated Jesus to visit Zaccheus' house for a meal.

Respect is the secret to long-lasting friendships.

Think about your own life for a moment. Those who respect you are the people you love to spend time with. They are the ones who receive your attention, your time, your love. On the other hand, you probably withdraw from those who have shown you disrespect in some way.

THEY REMEMBER MY NAME

"Hello, Dr. Murdock. So good to see you again!"

With these words I am always greeted at one of my favorite restaurants in Dallas. The owner always makes me feel special and respected. Naturally, I love it. His kindness is part of a magnetism that draws me back.

However, I have visited restaurants where I was treated as a nuisance, an interruption in their day. When I asked for A-1 Sauce to flavor my steak, they made me feel as though I'd committed the unpardonable sin! Needless to say, I rarely return to those places.

What we truly respect we ultimately attract.

THIS SAME PRINCIPLE APPLIES TO MIRACLES AND BLESSINGS

I heard a television host one night make sarcastic remarks about preachers who pray for the sick and believe in miracles. He sneered as he labeled them "faith healers."

Defiantly, he remarked, "I've never had a miracle or healing in *my* life."

He displayed complete disrespect for ministers of God who believed in miracles. I couldn't help but think of this principle of respect. It possibly explained why this man had not experienced miracles. *How could he attract miracles when he had no regard for them?*

As my friend Richard Roberts says, "He will start believing in miracles when he truly needs one!"

Do you *appreciate* blessings from God? If so, you will respect MEN OF GOD. They are God's *gifts* to the world to help unlock our faith for miracles. This is one of the reasons I support a number of ministries every month. It is my way of showing God that I respect them and His ministry through them.

So predictably, people who slander and criticize faith ministries may experience fewer miracles and blessings in their own lives.

DO YOU DISLIKE PHYSICAL EXERCISE?

If you're like me, you can think of many things you would rather do than follow a daily regimen of physical exercise.

Perhaps no one has ever motivated you to eat properly and exercise consistently. You simply have not learned the importance of maintaining good health. Consequently, when you face a sickness, you may find it difficult to use your faith because good health has never been a priority to you.

God began to show me this in my own life. I couldn't abuse my body and expect it to keep functioning properly. If I *really* wanted good health, I had to begin *respecting* my body. It deserved my time and effort, when I was *well* as much as when I was sick!

It was not an easy task for me. I knew I should begin walking or jogging daily and develop a routine of exercises. But something within me kept rebelling. I became puzzled and frustrated at myself.

Then one day it dawned on me. Back in my high school days, the coaches used extra laps and extra pushups as *punishment* for us. *So I subconsciously equated exercise as punishment.* This stirred up the resentment I had known as a teenager.

I had to change my opinion and *create a new respect* for physical fitness. I had to see exercise as a stepping stone to happiness instead of a punishment to my body. I had to rebuild my respect for a healthy body.

Maybe you are having a similar problem. Perhaps a sickness, a weakness, or even an overweight condition has haunted you throughout your life. It may require a little additional effort on your part to build a healthy respect for God's "temple" – your body, but it is worth your time and effort to be whole, healthy and fully alive again.

That same principle of respect operates in your personal finances.

A LETTER THAT SHOCKED ME

I received a letter recently that was rather startling.

"When we saw you several months ago on television you were teaching on prosperity. Frankly, my husband and I were turned off. We refused to watch your program, 'The Way Of The Winner,' until you started speaking on another subject. We have really been blessed this month through your teaching on the hurt and healing of divorce."

The letter continued, "I wish we had enough money to buy your book, *The Winner's World*, but we don't have anything left after our bills are paid. Here is our best offering we can afford at this time."

Taped to the letter was a quarter.

Here's what disturbed me. The woman who wrote said she and her husband were so poor they could scarcely pay their bills. They could not afford even to pay a few dollars for my book. They were unable to give more than 25 cents to the work of God! *Yet they became upset at me for teaching the laws of supply and blessing!*

Such reasoning amazed me. Here I was trying to help them *use their faith for FINANCES* and it angered them. But this is often typical of those who struggle in the throes of misfortune. Feeling inferior and intimidated because of their lack, people often become critical and disrespectful toward the very message they need and toward ministers God has sent to them.

You must respect the things in life that you want to attract.

When I was young, I remember taking drives with friends through wealthy neighborhoods of our town. Often, someone would say, "See that nice home? The people who live there are probably miserable."

Envy usually creates resentment. For that reason the poor sometimes feel hostile toward the wealthy, rather than learn from them.

Sometimes our background teaching has programmed us to feel *guilty* about desiring money and nice things, so we fail to attract them.

I know this has been controversial in some circles, but revolutionary principles are not always easily understood at first.

The bottom line is the Word of God, not the opinions of uninformed men. And, the Scriptures teach that wealth and riches come from the hand of God.

"But thou shalt remember the LORD thy God: for it is he that giveth thee power to get wealth, that he may establish his covenant which he sware unto thy fathers, as it is this day" (Deuteronomy 8:18).

WHEN YOU FACE ADVERSITY

Sometimes adversity will tempt you to lower a high standard of faith and change what you have been believing. This can paralyze your pursuit of your God-given dream.

DON'T REWRITE YOUR THEOLOGY TO ACCOMMODATE A TRAGEDY.

Your misfortune is always *temporary.* It is only for a *season.* Pain passes. Principles are permanent. The Word of God is settled forever.

"weeping may endure for a night, but joy cometh in the morning" (Psalm 30:5b).

This happened to me several years ago. I woke up one morning without a family, without a home, without furnishings, without a penny in the bank. Waves of hopelessness swept over me like ocean swells, leaving me confused and disheartened. As my friend Jamie Buckingham says, "I didn't know *what* I believed. I only knew in WHOM I believed."

It took months of waiting on God and an intense search of Scriptures before my life began to turn around. I had to make a decision. I could lower my goals and compromise my dreams – or fight to keep my DREAM SEED alive and vibrant within me. *If Satan can blur or blot out your DREAM SEED — that invisible photograph of a desired miracle – he will destroy you and God's dream in you will die.*

I must tell you, it was one of the most painful battles in my entire life. The scars of my divorce were carved deep within me. I fought every demon in hell 24 hours a day. Satan taunted me, "You are an absolute failure. You are crazy if you think you will ever succeed in the ministry."

Needing reassurance of God's call on my life, I read popular books by Christian counselors and even attended widely acclaimed seminars for help. These writers taught that ministers who failed in their marriages ought to leave the ministry and place themselves "on the shelf" for a time. This merely echoed what Satan had already spoken to me. I was tempted to agree.

For I, too, had always wanted to be the perfect preacher, with a perfect wife and perfect children, doing perfect things.

So, I began making plans to leave the ministry. I felt that God was through using me, and decided to go into business to support other preachers whom I admired, whom I thought were more "qualified" to represent the Gospel.

But one nagging thought persisted: my DREAM SEED. *I couldn't shake my calling.* I really can't explain it. Even as I write these words I am overwhelmed with the memories of those emotions. I just know that I kept *picturing* myself reaching out to brokenhearted, hurting people who were just like me. Bruised. Fragmented. Who desperately needed mending and reassurance of their worth. Somehow, I knew that this ministry would be needed. Needed by those whose hearts had been torn and dreams ripped apart.

No, God had never changed His original plan for me. Every demon in hell could not extract it from the soil of my spirit.

I decided to stay in the ministry. Regardless of the cost. I knew that too many people were hurting just like me. Broken marriages and devastating financial setbacks have crushed the dreams of multitudes. *I determined to fight back.*

As my feelings poured from me, I penned songs such as "You Can Make It," "I am Blessed," and "Jesus, Just The Mention Of Your Name."

Slowly it began to happen. Those dark clouds surrounding my DREAM SEED began to vanish. The sun began to shine again. My ministry weathered the storm, and grew even more effective through the daily radio programs and weekly telecasts, "The Way of the Winner."

DREAM SEEDS

What is YOUR DREAM SEED today? What miracle picture has God planted within YOUR heart? What desired blessing *dominates* your mind? If you truly *respect* it, it will inevitably come toward you.

Remember this: WHAT YOU TRULY RESPECT, YOU WILL ULTIMATELY ATTRACT.

The Master Key of
DESIRE

Principle: The proof of desire is pursuit.

The Master Key of Desire

Your DREAM SEED must be something that you truly desire.

You see, men rarely reach for what they *need*; but they will *always* reach for what they really *want*.

If you truly desire miracles and blessings in your life, you must be willing to *reach* for them. I've always said, "The grapes of blessing are never placed within your mouth; they are simply placed within your reach."

God respects a reacher.

God rewards a reacher.

I don't quite agree with the time worn adage, "Necessity is the mother of invention." Rather, I believe that *desire* is what gives birth to miracles.

Our desires are far more motivating than our needs.

It was *desire* that inspired the Wright brothers to fly. It was *desire* that motivated Thomas Edison to persist through 10,000 experiments that failed before perfecting the incandescent light bulb.

DESIRE AND HENRY FORD

The persistence of Henry Ford is legendary. A popular story tells of his desire to create an engine with all eight cylinders cast in one block.

Every engineer who worked for him insisted it was impossible. However, Ford instructed them to pursue his project anyway and remain on the job until they succeeded.

Six months later, nothing had changed. One year later, those same engineers shook their heads dejectedly.

"It's just impossible, Mr. Ford," they said.

But Henry Ford possessed the *determination* and *desire* to succeed. He pressed them to continue. And suddenly it happened. The secret was discovered, and the famous V-8 motor became a reality. Ford's unwavering *desire* revolutionized the automobile industry.

HOW STRONG IS YOUR DESIRE?

How intense is your craving for your DREAM SEED to happen?

Do you *hate* being poor? You must despise where you are before you will ever be where you want to be.

THE PROOF OF DESIRE IS PURSUIT.

GOD, ME AND THE SAXOPHONE

I have always enjoyed listening to saxophone music. For many years I told my friends, "Oh, I'd love to play the saxophone. I would give anything to learn how to play."

After talking this way for some years, one day something inside me seemed to say, *"Why don't you take lessons?"*

"I don't want to take lessons," I argued.

"Then shut up and stop telling everyone you want to play the saxophone," was the inner response.

YOU SEE, WHAT I AM WILLING TO INVEST MY TIME AND MONEY TOWARD REVEALS WHAT I REALLY WANT.

The *real proof* of my desire is what I am willing to *pursue*.

What do you love *talking* about? What *books* excite you? What receives your *time* and *attention*? What *dominates* your thoughts?

What you think about the most is what you have chosen to master you. Your job, children, or mate – or yes, your DREAM SEED.

There are two Scriptures that have helped me understand the power of desire.

"Delight thyself also in the LORD; and he shall give thee the desires of thine heart" (Psalm 37:4).

"What things soever ye desire, when ye pray, believe that ye receive them, and ye shall have them" (Mark 11:24).

You must possess more than a need for your miracle. You must possess true *desire*; desire enough to *reach*.

MY FRIEND AND THE PENNY

A funny thing happened several years ago with a friend of mine. As we walked down the street together, he was expressing his annoyance at preachers who were "always talking about money."

"But money is important," I reasoned with him. "Don't you think about money?"

"I never think about money!" he retorted.

I smiled and thought to myself, *he's either a fool or a liar!*

As we approached a curb, my friend suddenly spied a penny lying on the pavement. Like a deep-sea diver, he dove for the coin.

I nearly burst out laughing. I was glad it wasn't a quarter. I might have lost him into the pavement.

The point is, *we will always reach for what we really desire.* Whether we admit it or not. Unfortunately many of us are like my friend. *We often dive for the pennies of life instead of reaching for the high quality principles that God has intended for us to live by.*

"Let the LORD be magnified, which hath pleasure in the prosperity of his servant" (Psalm 35:27b).

Your desire will always make you go the *extra* mile, *push* a little harder, *reach* a little higher.

Look at this fascinating picture in Mark 5.

A certain woman had been afflicted with an issue of blood for 12 years. She had spent all her money on physicians, and her condition had merely gotten worse.

But she carried the seed of desire within her. She wanted to be healed. And, she believed that if she could touch the garment of Jesus, she would be made whole.

The woman probably was in great pain. Undoubtedly, the thronging crowd made it nearly impossible for her to reach Jesus. But she made it. She touched Him! *(When you want something badly enough, you will somehow find a way to get it.)*

"And straightway the fountain of her blood was dried up; and she felt in her body that she was healed of that plague" (Mark 5:29).

Her *need* (or sickness) had to bow to her DESIRE, (the miracle of her healing). Her DESIRE became the MASTER of her *need*. She forced need to whimper at the feet of desire. Desire won, and healing came.

Friend, please believe me today.

You *can* defeat sickness. You *can* conquer poverty. And it all begins with that intense burning *desire* within you.

HOW TO FUEL THE FIRE OF YOUR DESIRES

God has planted within you the seeds of desire for good things. Now you must concentrate on watering and nurturing the *growth* of those seeds.

God planted the desire for a son deep within Abraham, but Abraham had to *use* his faith to make it happen. Desires are like people. They are *born*, they *grow*, and they can *die*.

There are three major ways you can feed the desire for your DREAM.

1. VISUALIZATION — *Sustaining the Mental Photograph of what you want to receive from God.*

In Mark 5, the woman carried a DREAM SEED in her heart and mind of her healing. "If I may touch but his clothes," she said, "I shall be made whole." *She ignored the distraction* of the crowd and REACHED for the dream within her – and RECEIVED her miracle.

YOU WILL NEVER ACCOMPLISH A GREAT DREAM WITHOUT A BURNING DESIRE FOR IT. You must *feed* that desire *daily*. You do this by continually visualizing the *rewards* and *pleasures* of its attainment.

Yes, visualization will fuel the fires of your desire for your DREAM SEED.

2. ASSOCIATIONS — *Wholesome relationships that create a momentum toward your DREAM SEED.*

It is exceedingly important to have the right kind of friends. Many people have lost motivation for their DREAM SEED because they associated with faithless and foolish people.

"He that walketh with wise men shall be wise: but a companion of fools shall be destroyed" (Proverbs 13:20).

Don't expose your 16 x 20 DREAM SEED to 5 x 7 mentalities around you. Disregard unkind words of critics. Don't dignify their slander by repeating it. Criticism is usually the death gargle of a non-achiever anyway.

Dare to reach for the companionship of great thinkers. *Invest* in their books. *Listen* to their teaching cassettes. *Absorb* their spirit and victorious attitudes that have driven them to great achievement.

3. CONCENTRATION — *Focusing on the completion of one worthwhile goal at a time.*

One of the most important things I have ever learned is to *give total attention to one thing at a time.* Many people allow their creativity to scatter their attention. Their abilities become lost through misfocus.

Your creativity is a gift. Don't let it become your enemy. Harness it. It is better to *complete* one worthwhile goal than *to begin* ten others.

Everyone will clamor for your attention.

And, as harsh as it may seem, you must learn to dismiss from your presence those people who distract you from a God-inspired goal. Remember, your DREAM SEED deserves your *undivided* attention.

Now, let's examine one of the explosive gifts God has given you – your IMAGINATION.

The Master Key of
IMAGINATION

Principle: You will always move in the
direction of your strongest and
most dominate thought.

The Master Key of Imagination

The third key that unlocks the incredible potential of your DREAM SEED is your *imagination*.

Your imagination is an invisible machine inside your mind. God gave it to you to *create pictures*. Pictures of those things you *desire*.

One of the most beautiful gifts God has given you is your *mind*. There are two major functions of your mind. One is your *memory*, the other is your *imagination*. Both are God-given gifts that can help or hurt you. Your MEMORY will *photograph, file* and *replay* pictures of your *past*. Your IMAGINATION, on the other hand, *creates and preplays pictures of things you want to happen in your future*.

Great achievers usually have learned to *replay* the memories of their past *triumphs* and *preplay* the pictures of *their desired successes*.

For example, when David faced the giant Goliath, he mentally *replayed* his previous victories in killing the bear and the lion. Then he used his imagination to *picture* and *preplay* his impending victory over Goliath.

WHERE DO MIRACLES BEGIN?

I believe miracles begin in the soil of your *imagination*. God plants your DREAM SEED within you. Then, that DREAM SEED is *incubated* in the room of your imagination.

Abraham carried a DREAM SEED planted by God. It was a picture of countless generations of children.

"And I will make thy seed as the dust of the earth: so that if a man can number the dust of the earth, then shall thy seed also be numbered" (Genesis 13:16).

"And I will make thy seed to multiply as the stars of heaven" (Genesis 26:4a).

Abraham used his IMAGINATION to *strengthen his faith.* Yes, he was human, like you and me. He fought a constant stream of doubts regarding his DREAM SEED. His wife, Sarah, 90-years-old and long past her childbearing years, even laughed! *Their faith for a son did not happen overnight.* But they carried the DREAM SEED in their *imagination*, and Isaac was conceived.

THE POWER OF YOUR IMAGINATION

A fascinating story in Genesis 11 illustrates the power of imagination. The Babylonians wanted to build a city with a tower that would reach into Heaven. Apparently, it was an exaltation *against* God. He was displeased. So He confused their tongues and scattered them abroad.

But there's a remarkable observation in Genesis 11:6 about these people and their ability to *picture* the goals they had set for themselves. *"And the LORD said, Behold, the people is one, and they have all one language; and this they begin to do: AND NOW NOTHING WILL BE RESTRAINED FROM THEM, WHICH THEY HAVE IMAGINED TO DO."*

God *acknowledged* the gift and the power of imagination He had given to them. Unfortunately, they had chosen to misuse it.

He has given every one of us this incredible gift – *the ability to picture within our minds something we want to happen*, knowing we will ultimately move toward its fulfillment.

YOUR WIFE AND BLOOMINGDALE'S

Your imagination can unleash unexpected energy. I'm sure you've seen a similar scenario at your house....

You arrive home from work. Your wife is sprawled on the sofa, appearing totally exhausted.

"Honey, what are we having for supper tonight?" you ask.

"Oh, Marcus, I can't prepare supper tonight," she replies. "It's been a really terrible day at the office. My feet are killing me. My back is acting up again, and I feel a migraine coming on. Would you mind fixing something for yourself?"

You stumble around the kitchen, opening the refrigerator and searching for something to satisfy your hunger pangs.

Suddenly, the phone rings.

"Hi, Marcus, this is Tammie. May I speak to Jena?" asks the voice on the other end.

"Well, Tammie, she's really too tired to talk to anyone right now, but I will tell her you called."

"Oh, Marcus, this is too important. Please let me talk to her for just one minute," Tammie implores.

So you call your wife. "Tammie's on the phone for you. She says it's important."

Sluggishly, your wife gropes for the telephone. "Yes, Tammie?" she mutters.

"Oh, Jena, you won't believe it. Do you remember that gorgeous red dress we saw last week at Bloomingdale's? They have just marked all those dresses down to half price. For tonight only! You've got to go with me!"

Instantly, your wife leaps to her feet. "Oh, my, yes, Tammie!" she exclaims. "I'll be ready in 20 minutes."

You stand in the kitchen, stunned, as your wife sweeps like a tornado into the bedroom, shouting over her shoulder, "Oh, honey, this is what I've been waiting for. You're going to love this dress! They're having a half-price sale till 9 tonight. I just have to go!" And before you can grab your checkbook, she's gone like Elijah the Second in a whirlwind!

Was your wife exaggerating her fatigue and weariness earlier?

Probably not. But a *new photograph* had been placed in her mind. A different picture had suddenly *dominated her imagination*, instantly creating new energy and motivation. It happens to all of us, doesn't it?

God has given you the gift of your imagination. He wants you to use your imagination productively. So start now and grow the seeds of good health, favor, faith and financial prosperity in the soil of your imagination. Those DREAM SEEDS will fire your enthusiasm and cause miracles and blessings to flow into your life. Yes, even beyond anything you've ever dreamed or imagined.

JESUS SAW BEYOND THE CROSS

Jesus was acquainted with sorrow. He knew pain. He experienced rejection. But something kept drawing Him toward the cross.

Or, did He see something *beyond* the cross?

"Looking unto Jesus the author and finisher of our faith; who FOR THE JOY THAT WAS SET BEFORE HIM endured the cross, despising the shame, and is set down at the right hand of the throne of God" (Hebrews 12:2).

His mind was on the *Resurrection*, not just Calvary.

He endured the pain of the Cross by concentrating on *what was to follow* His death.

His *focus was the Resurrection* on the OTHER side of the Crucifixion. It was evident that *Heaven was often on His mind* while He was on earth.

"In my Father's house are many mansions: if it were not so, I would have told you. I go to prepare a place for you" (John 14:2).

Some call it goal-setting...visualization...imaging. You may call it anything you will. But it is a basic law in achieving great successes. *Your life will always move in the direction of your dominant thought.*

Your imagination is the workshop of your mind. You can DREAM, DESIGN, and DETERMINE what you want to happen in your life. Whatever dominates your imagination *today* will very likely be experienced in your life *tomorrow.*

WINNING ATHLETES USE THEIR IMAGINATIONS

A major university conducted an experiment with its basketball team. They divided 10 men into two teams to determine an average percentage of free throws scored. Team A was instructed to practice free throws for an hour each day for 30 consecutive days.

However, Team B had a different assignment. The men were told to remain in the locker room and, *using their imagination only*, VISUALIZE themselves shooting free throws and mentally *picturing* the basketball dropping through the net. This *imaging* was to be practiced for the same time period as Team A – one hour daily for 30 consecutive days.

The results were remarkable.

Members of Team A, after actually practicing on the court every day, improved their free throw score by 23 percent. Member of Team B, *using only their imaginations* for 30 days, improved their score by 22 percent! Almost identical improvement! It's hard to believe, isn't it?

YOUR IMAGINATION CONTROLS YOU.

"...whatsoever thing are true, whatsoever things are honest, whatsoever things are just, whatsoever things are pure, whatsoever things are lovely, whatsoever things are of good report; if there be any virtue, and if there be any praise, think on these things" (Philippians 4:8).

PROTECT YOUR MIND AND IMAGINATION

Thoughts will invade your imagination from almost everywhere. Thoughts of *fear* and *unbelief* are what I call *disaster seeds* planted by Satan.

Thoughts of *miracles* and *blessings* are DREAM SEEDS planted by God.

Your imagination is *not* a referee. It will not judge whether the seeds going into your mind are good or bad. It will simply *grow* whatever seeds you decide to water and nurture.

This is one of the reasons we need the Holy Spirit and the Word of God in our lives. The Holy Spirit will help you harness and focus your imagination to grow your DREAM SEED planted by God.

YOU CAN CHANGE DISASTER SEEDS TO DREAM SEEDS.

In 1 Kings 17, God sent the prophet Elijah to the home of an impoverished widow.

"What are we having for supper tonight?" he asked the woman.

"Two pancakes for me and my boy, and then we are going to die," she replied. (This is the Mike Murdock version, of course!)

She had a Disaster Seed: a *picture* of her approaching *starvation*.

Elijah, however, had a DREAM SEED: a *picture* of her *supply*.

He said, "Give me a meal first...." Then he added, "Your meal barrel will never run dry."

Elijah planted a DREAM SEED of supply in her *imagination* to help *stimulate her faith*.

God sent Elijah to paint a DREAM SEED on the walls of her mind – a *picture* of SUPPLY *instead of her starvation*. That DREAM SEED – the invisible photograph of her needed supply – *unleashed* her faith and gave her an incredible miracle of provision during the famine.

YOUR IMAGINATION'S MATE — YOUR MEMORY

Your memory keeps files of the past: photographs of past *painful* experiences and those of past *pleasurable* experiences.

I am sure that you can remember many *pleasurable experiences* in your past. You can probably remember the day you were married or received your high-school diploma or the day you passed the test for your first driver's license. I am sure you can well remember the moment you gave your life to Christ.

Replaying these past triumphs and victories in your mind is a powerful way to *motivate* yourself toward your DREAM SEED.

David did this when he faced Goliath. He replayed his memory of victory over the lion and the bear. His *mental rehearsal* ignited the fire of courage within him to face and conquer the giant Goliath.

On the other hand, be careful in conversations and associations with people who provoke painful memories.

One of the most productive life-principles in the writings of Paul is found in Philippians 3:13, 14: *"...forgetting those things which are behind, and reaching forth unto those things which are before, I press toward the mark for the prize of the high calling of God in Christ Jesus."*

The prophet Isaiah commanded the same principle of forgetting.

"Remember ye not the former things, neither consider the things of old. Behold I will do a new thing; now it shall spring forth; shall ye not know it? I will even make a way in the wilderness, and rivers in the desert" (Isaiah 43:18,19).

The *healing* of your memories will not remove your ability to recall your past, but rather give you the ability to *replay* the past *without the accompanying pain.*

Joseph experienced this in Genesis 42. He *recognized* his brothers who had wronged him in his past, but he felt no animosity toward them. He had discerned the *purpose* of the pain and realized that God had actually *used* his unfortunate experience to *promote* him!

BEGIN USING YOUR IMAGINATION PRODUCTIVELY

Every great achiever has used the Master Key of Imagination to unlock the door to his miracles and blessings. God wants you to use *your* imagination the same way.

Your marriage is being restored. *Picture it.*

Your memory is being healed. *Picture it.*

The healing power of Jesus is flowing through your body this very moment. *Receive it.*

Money is being placed in your hands to pay your bills. *Expect it.* Your Heavenly Father wants to bless you beyond anything you have ever experienced.

Oh, will you dare to believe this? Will you dare to shake off the mistakes of the *past* – and *reach* for the miracles God desires to place in your hands?

YOU CAN CHANGE WHAT HAS BEEN HAPPENING IN YOUR LIFE. You can *reverse* yesterday's wrong decision by making a *good* decision today. You can turn the tide. *Nothing is impossible.* NOTHING.

Jesus said, "If thou canst believe, all things are possible to him that believeth" (Mark 9:23).

REFUSE THE CHAINS OF PAST INJUSTICES. Don't waste your time analyzing those who have wronged you. Use your energy to create new roads ahead of you, not repairing the old roads behind you! Start *focusing* on your own *immediate* goals and the DREAM SEED ahead God has planted within you.

DON'T MISUSE YOUR IMAGINATION

Some people *misuse* and *misdirect* their imagination. They feed their imaginations destructive pictures, *Disaster Seeds.* This happened in Noah's generation.

"And GOD saw that the wickedness of man was great in the earth, and that every imagination of the thoughts of his heart was only evil continually" (Genesis 6:5).

The Apostle Paul recognized its misuse.

"Because that, when they knew God, they glorified him not as God, neither were thankful; but became vain in their imaginations, and their foolish heart was darkened" (Romans 1:21).

DEALING WITH DISASTER SEEDS

Each of us face daily temptations. Advertisers stir and awaken our physical appetites via billboards, magazines and television. Overeating has almost become a way of life in America. Illicit sexual gratification is promoted in the same manner.

These *pictures* are *planted* as *seeds* into our minds and imaginations continually. These seed-pictures are *destructive.* I call them Disaster Seeds because they destroy your faith in God. They must be confronted and uprooted from the soil of your imagination.

"Casting down imaginations, and every high thing that exalteth itself against the knowledge of God, and bringing into captivity every thought to the obedience of Christ" (2 Corinthians 10:5).

Your imagination will grow any seed that you plant in it. Good or bad. This is why David said, *"I will set no wicked thing before mine eyes"* (Psalm 101:3).

He rejected from his imagination *any person* or *picture* that could be a *distraction* to his desired goals.

Jesus warned about these Disaster Seeds entering through the eye-gate.

"The light of the body is the eye: if therefore thine eye be single, thy whole body shall be full of light. But if thine eye be evil, thy while body shall be full of the darkness. If therefore the light that is in thee be darkness, how great is that darkness!" (Matthew 6:22,23).

Remember, your imagination is the room of incubation for your seeds of faith. And you can experience unlimited miracles when you allow God to rule your imagination.

FROM THE PIT TO THE PALACE

Joseph, in Genesis, received a DREAM SEED from God. He *chose to believe it*, and saw himself destined for the throne. His brothers hated him for it, and planted seeds of confusion, hatred and jealously into his life.

But Joseph refused to nurture those Disaster Seeds of unforgiveness and hostility. He refused to doubt his DREAM SEED, and the years of watering that DREAM SEED in his imagination eventually promoted him from slave boy to prime minister.

WHAT GOD DID FOR JOSEPH HE CAN DO FOR YOU. You may be misunderstood by someone close to you right now. Bitter words may have been hurled at you this very day. You may feel like giving up your dreams. Those are normal feelings we all have occasionally.

But I pray for you, my friend, in the precious name of Jesus, this very moment that your DREAM SEED will be ignited again. *What God spoke to you in the light, don't you dare doubt in the darkness.*

Make up your mind to stand your ground. DARE TO DREAM AGAIN. Start dreaming *bigger* than you've ever dreamed before. Just like Joseph chose to grow the DREAM SEED from God, you, too, can start growing the DREAM SEED God has planted within you.

The Master Key of
GOAL-SETTING

Principle: You must know what you want
before your creative faith can
target toward it.

The Master Key of Goal-Setting

For more than two decades I have traveled around the world, meeting the greatest achievers of my generation.

An obvious trait that each of them has in common is the routine practice of goal-setting. *Writing down their goals has become part of their lifestyle.* In fact, many of them actually sit down and make a detailed list of their exact dreams and a step-by-step plan of how they intend to accomplish them.

JESUS RESPECTED THIS KIND OF GOAL-SETTING. He respected men who thought enough of their dreams to create plans for their attainment. *God loves a PLANNER.*

Noah had a plan for the Ark.

Moses had a plan for the Tabernacle.

Solomon had a plan for the Temple.

And most important of all they accepted the instructions of God for their projects. As Jesus Himself taught, *"For which of you, intending to build a tower, sitteth not down first, and counteth the cost, whether he have sufficient to finish it?"* (Luke 14:28).

Even the common ant is considered wise for *preparing* for the future.

"Go to the ant, thou sluggard; consider her ways, and be wise: Which having no guide, overseer, or ruler, Provideth her meat in the summer, and gathereth her food in the harvest" (Proverbs 6:6-8).

While you may not have your D.M.B. (Desired Miracle or Blessing) written down on paper yet, it should already be clearly engraved on the tablets of your heart.

You will never leave where you are right now until you know exactly where you want to be. You must know exactly where you want to be. You must know what you really want before you can obtain it. YOU WILL NEVER CHANGE YOUR LOCATION UNTIL YOU DETERMINE YOUR DESTINATION.

The story of the blind beggar in Luke 18 presents a good example. He sat by the wayside begging. When he asked those around him about the noise of the multitude passing by, he was told that Jesus of Nazareth was walking through Jericho.

When he heard it was Jesus, the blind man cried out, "Jesus, thou Son of David, have mercy on me!" Those nearby tried to silence the man. Always remember: *Those who have not suffered your darkness cannot truly understand your craving for light.* He simply cried out again. "Jesus, thou Son of David, have mercy on me!" *He knew what he wanted and nothing was going to stop him from reaching for it.*

GREAT THINGS ALWAYS HAPPEN TO THOSE WHO PERSIST. Winners are people who are willing to try *one more time.*

As my friend Don Cox says, *"Those who KEEP ON asking shall receive...those who KEEP ON seeking shall find...and those who KEEP ON knocking shall find the doors opening."*

Jesus commanded them to bring the blind man to Him. Then Jesus asked, "What do you want Me to do for you?"

The blind man replied, "Lord, that I may receive my sight."

Why did Jesus ask the man what he wanted? His need appeared obvious. But the principle of agreement is one of the intrinsic laws of God: *You must know what you really want before God will give it to you.*

A covenant of agreement requires two or more people.

"if two you shall agree on earth as touching any thing that they shall ask, it shall be done for them of my Father which is in heaven" (Matthew 18:19).

JESUS ALWAYS RESPONDS TO PEOPLE WHO KNOW WHAT THEY WANT. The woman in Mark 5 knew what she wanted. She had established a *goal*. She was determined to touch the hem of the garment of Christ. She reached Him – and *received* the miracle she desired.

The fact that God has given you a DREAM SEED – a clear mental picture of a goal or miracle you want to obtain – healing, finances, a personal ministry, whatever He has placed in your spirit – is an indication that it exists! *The persistent presence of a God-given desire in your heart is proof that it is possible for you to attain it.*

God wouldn't give geese a desire to fly south if there was no south to fly toward! *You cannot out dream God.* You cannot create something in your mind that God cannot produce. The *creation* cannot out perform our *Creator*.

You may be feeling inadequate, inferior and incapable of accomplishing your dreams. But God gave you your DREAM SEED for a *purpose*.

What is the BIGGEST miracle you need in your life right now? What *specific* blessings have you been asking God to give you? Is it a better job? A new home? A physical healing? NAME what you want from God.

You see, your faith cannot be released until you have established a clear-cut target and goal.

DO YOU HAVE ANY DEBTS?

Dale and Pam were a young couple in desperate financial trouble. They came to my office depressed and totally disillusioned with life. Over their heads in debt, they just could not seem to get their lives together. They decided to file for bankruptcy and wanted my suggestions.

"How much do you owe your creditors right now?" I asked.

"Thousands of dollars," Dale said dejectedly.

"Tell me *exactly* how much you owe," I insisted.

Finally they confessed that they didn't know the exact amount. They didn't even have a budget. They had never sat down with a financial planner to establish a payoff schedule of their bills. Believe it or not, they didn't even know the amount of finances necessary for their needs each week.

Consequently, their faith didn't have a specific target to focus upon.

You see, it's difficult to use your faith for $400 a week if you don't even know that you *need* $400 a week!

You simply must set goals. You must have a goal to *measure progress.*

Remember, God respects people who plan like Noah, Moses and Solomon.

God is a thinker. He is the Master Organizer. He is not an emotional tyrant bungling His way through His Universe. The fact that He has scheduled the Marriage Supper of the Lamb 6,000 years *in advance* is proof that He is definitely organized!

And He has a *plan* for *your* miracle. God responds to you when you know what you want – chart your course toward it.

I was appalled recently by a Christian television guest who mocked ministers with "little magic formulas for miracles."

"There are no special formulas that make miracles happen," he said. "Who are we to tell God what He will or will not do? Blessings and Miracles are sovereign acts by a sovereign God. God alone chooses who and when He will bless, and there is nothing any of us can do about it."

I shook my head in disbelief when I heard this. This disastrous philosophy insinuates that rebellion is never punished, nor obedience rewarded. Also, the man had overlooked an obvious fact: Our world is wondrously *planned*. The human body, intricate and incredible, has order and structure. Only a fool would fail to recognize God as a thinking and organized Creator. And it only follows that He has formulas, plans, and methods for our miracles.

MIRACLES SHOULD NOT BE MYSTERIES

There are reasons why miracles and blessings happen to us.

You know that laws and principles govern this universe. You may not always know the exact combination, but the *existence of a lock* is PROOF *that a key exists somewhere.*

One of those Master Keys to unlocking your DREAM SEED is *goal-setting.* God wants you to *focus* the desire of your heart and *use your faith* for its attainment.

What do you *think* about most of the time? What outstanding miracle do you *long for?* A healing in your body? A million-dollar business deal? The restoration of your marriage? Salvation for a loved one?

Then *establish* your goal, *discern* God's plan for its attainment – and STEP OUT IN FAITH TOWARD IT!

The Master Key of
OBEDIENCE

Principle: God will never advance you
instructions beyond your last
act of disobedience.

The Master Key of Obedience

I feel particularly concerned that you understand this Master Key. Frankly, I believe obedience is one of the most important of the seven Master Keys to your DREAM SEED.

Obedience is *doing anything God asks you to do, regardless of its cost or consequences.* These instructions, or commands from God may come to you through His *Word*, through the inner voice of the *Holy Spirit* or through a qualified *man* of God. Any act or attitude of rebellion will instantly *paralyze* your progress toward your DREAM SEED. God never sends *additional* messages to us until the previous messages have been obeyed.

A principle of obedience is this: GOD WILL NEVER GIVE ADVANCE INSTRUCTIONS BEYOND YOUR LAST ACT OF DISOBEDIENCE.

Let's talk a moment about the will of God for your life.

TWO PARTS OF THE WILL OF GOD

I feel that there are two parts of the will of God. One is what I call the "FOREVER" will of God; the other I call the "NOW" will of God.

You see, some of His commands are permanent, eternal and intended for *every* human being at *all times.* For instance, *all* men are commanded to *repent* of their sins. Salvation is *always* the will of God for man. *"And the times of this ignorance God winked at: but now commandeth all men every where to repent"* (Acts 17:30).

It is *always* God's will and desire for men to *repent* and *be restored to fellowship.* The ten commandments are universal as well. These unchanging, permanent instructions recorded in the Scriptures are what I call the FOREVER will of God.

Another example of the FOREVER will of God is the *healing of our sicknesses.*

"Beloved, I wish above all things that thou mayest prosper and be in health, even as thy soul prospereth" (3 John 2).

"But He was wounded for our transgressions, he was bruised for our iniquities: the chastisement of our peace was upon him; and with his stripes we are healed" (Isaiah 53:5).

TOTAL FORGIVENESS is also a FOREVER will of God toward you.

"Bless the Lord, O my soul, and forget not all his benefits: Who forgiveth all thine iniquities; who healeth all thy diseases" (Psalm 103:2,3).

"As far as the east is from the west, so far hath he removed our transgressions from us" (Psalm 103:12).

"But the mercy of the Lord is from everlasting to everlasting upon them that fear him, and his righteousness unto children's children; To such as keep his covenant, and to those that remember his commandments to do them" (Psalm 103:17).

It is the FOREVER will of God for man to *praise and worship God.*

"I will bless the Lord at all times: his praise shall continually be in my mouth" (Psalm 34:1).

Forgiving others is a FOREVER will of God.

Has anyone in your life wronged you? Your willingness to forgive them is a FOREVER will of God. It is also an act of obedience that can unlock your DREAM SEED.

HOW TO FORGIVE YOUR WAY TO A MIRACLE

In a fascinating story I learned about some years ago, a well-known minister related a miracle. It happened to a woman who had been bedridden for many years.

The minister prayed for her, along with many others, in a long healing line night after night. While others were raised from wheelchairs and many outstanding healings took place, somehow this one woman could not seem to receive her healing.

It really disturbed this great preacher. So, he sought God several hours each day for an answer. Each night he would come back to the crusade, yearning to see her healed. But for some unknown reason, he could not sense a flow of faith as he prayed for her.

Then something happened. As the crusade neared its closing, the preacher, on his way to the pulpit one night, walked by the woman. He noticed a sparkle in her eye that had not been there any other night.

"I'm going to receive my healing tonight," she exclaimed excitedly.

He almost pitied her. But *something* about the tone of her voice struck him, and he became convinced that this night was different.

This was going to be her night for a miracle.

At the close of his message, the minister prayed for the sick as usual. When he came to this particular woman, he stretched out his hands toward her. Suddenly, she *leaped from the wheelchair* she had occupied for many years. She was *instantly* healed by the power of God!

WHAT MADE THE DIFFERENCE?

"What in the world happened to you today?" the minister asked the woman. "I knew there was a difference in your voice and in your eyes. *What happened?*"

"As I was praying today," she answered, "I sensed that I had become bitter toward God because of my handicap. I also remembered a relative who had wronged me many years ago. I have harbored unforgiveness inside me for many years toward this relative."

"I realized I needed the love of God and His forgiveness more than I needed a miracle of healing. I *repented* of my bitterness, and as it left me, forgiveness began to flow out of me toward that relative. Somehow, that's when faith came into my heart for my deliverance. I just knew that tonight was my night for a miracle!"

Incredible, isn't it?

The woman's *obedience* and *willingness to forgive* UNLOCKED her own miracle. Her DREAM SEED, almost smothered by bitterness and unforgiveness, was *birthed* as she became *obedient* to the voice of the Holy Spirit.

"...What things soever ye desire, when ye pray, believe that ye receive them, and ye shall have them. And when ye stand praying forgive, if ye have ought against any: that your Father also which is in heaven may forgive you your trespasses.

But if ye do not forgive, neither will your Father which is in heaven forgive your trespasses" (Mark 11:24-26).

WHEN YOU FORGIVE OTHERS, GOD FORGIVES YOU.

Tithing is a "FOREVER" will of God.

Thousands are living in disobedience to this FOREVER will of God. Consciously or unconsciously they are breaking one of the greatest laws in the kingdom system.

"And all the tithe of the land, whether of the seed of the land, or of the fruit of the tree, is the LORD's: it is holy unto the LORD" (Leviticus 27:30).

"Bring ye all the tithes into the storehouse, that there may be meat in mine house, and prove me now herewith, saith the LORD of hosts..." (Malachi 3:10).

Remember, GOD WILL NOT ADVANCE YOU INSTRUCTIONS OR INFORMATION BEYOND YOUR LAST ACT OF DISOBEDIENCE. And beyond that point, every incoming message will be distorted. *You cannot progress beyond your last act of disobedience.*

This incredible principle is practically unknown among Christians today. God will not give you *current* instructions if you are rebelling against a FOREVER will of God.

THE "NOW" WILL OF GOD

The second part of obedience is what I call the NOW will of God. It is *personalized* instruction just for *you* relating to your *current circumstances*. These *individualized* directives are for you *only*, and are given as you need them.

A $50,000 BLESSING

I was still new in the ministry years ago when, unexpectedly, I received a cancellation of a two-week crusade. In those days, especially, a cancellation was a major blow financially.

"Churches, churches," I complained bitterly to God. "Why do they do this to me...what am I going to do?"

I was still fuming when the telephone rang. It was another pastor. And he wanted me to come for a two-week revival. Immediately.

"I'm sorry," I said, nursing my grudge. "I've got business to take care of back home next week." (Well, that was true!)

"We run only about 17 people," he continued. (Well, then I KNEW I wasn't going to accept!)

The pastor persisted. "Will you at least pray about it?" he asked finally.

"Sure, I'll pray about it," I replied, and then hung up the phone.

I began mumbling, "Lord, if you want me to go, just tell me." After a few minutes I began feeling that maybe I should put a little more effort into it.

I knelt down beside my bed in the little motel room. "God, do you want me to go?"

The answer came. Yes, I was to go.

I went to that little church of 17 people. I didn't feel like preaching when I got there, but God rewarded my *obedience.* Several made commitments to Christ, and several lifelong friendships were established. And, believe it or not, out of that tiny congregation God gave me some very special partners who contributed more than $50,000 to my ministry! Oh, never underestimate the importance God places on your obedience to Him!

OBEDIENCE. When you obey God, He blesses the work of your hands. No, He may not reveal *beforehand* all His rewards for your obedience. But, as you are faithful, He will give you more than you've ever dreamed possible.

Sometimes what God tells you to do will seem *illogical.* It may even *deprive* you of an immediate gratification. It may sometimes wound your pride. It may even appear unrelated to your miracle. *But it will inevitably and always be rewarded. AMPLY.*

SCARED AT SIX YEARS OLD

When I was a boy of six, my father pastored a church in Orange, Texas. I attended a school called Little Cypress, and had a teacher named Mrs. Ryder.

As the school year drew to a close, I remember how nervous I felt wondering whether I had passed or not on my report card.

I had studied and desperately hoped I would be promoted to the second grade, but I knew I had not done well in conduct. (In fact, I never did well in conduct my entire 12 years in school!)

The big day of reckoning came, and I remember grabbing my report card from Mrs. Ryder's hand and rushing outside to read my grades in private lest I had failed.

There – I spied the check mark. *PASSED!* My heart sang all the way home on the bus. I was ready for new information, promotion to the second grade.

We all accept this Life-Principle in *progress* and *promotion* throughout our lifetime. It holds true in school, college, career, the armed forces. And this REWARD SYSTEM is especially true in the kingdom of God.

God doesn't promote you according to your age. He doesn't promote you according to your I.Q. Nor does He promote you according to your abilities. *God promotes and rewards you according to your progressive acts of obedience.*

ARE YOU BEING ROBBED?

I am always saddened by television and newspaper accounts of families whose homes are burglarized and precious items stolen. Sometimes it takes these victims years of hard work to replace their losses. Tragically, it happens every day.

But there is something even worse: *When a man is robbed of his DREAM SEED.*

Millions are robbed of daily miracles because of their defiant and stubborn rebellion to a God-command.

Our disobedience disappoints the heart of God. It ties His hands. *God cannot commit Himself to the success of a rebel.* In fact, He warned Israel, *"Moreover, all these curses shall come upon thee, and shall pursue thee, and overtake thee, till thou be destroyed; because thou hearkenedst not unto the voice of the LORD thy God, to keep his commandments and his statutes which he commanded thee"* (Deuteronomy 28:45).

It is suicidal to play games with God. Every rebel will ultimately be penalized.

Please listen to me carefully. Can I be completely frank with you? It is difficult for me to write these paragraphs...they just don't seem to fit in with a book on miracles and blessings.

But I desperately want you to succeed. And I know that you cannot succeed and be totally happy with your life if you allow *one seed of rebellion* to exist within you. *Sin is a heartache to God.* You must *confront* it. You must *uproot* it. You must *ask* His forgiveness. It can happen *right now,* even as you are reading these words.

Would you pray this prayer aloud with me before you read any further?

"Dear Heavenly Father, I recognize sin in my life today, and I need your forgiveness. I thank You for Your Son, Jesus Christ, Who died on Calvary as a sacrifice for my sins. I believe that Your blood cleanses me today. I receive You as my Lord and Master and King who rules my life from this moment and forever. Amen."

Oh, friend, do you feel what I'm feeling this very moment? I feel the sweet presence of Jesus even now as I'm writing these words. *I feel as though I am sitting right there beside you.*

SOMETHING HAS JUST HAPPENED INSIDE YOUR HEART! You know that, too, don't you? And this is just the *beginning* of a great parade of miracles and blessings in your life! THIS MOMENT OF COMPLETE SURRENDER TO CHRIST CAN BE THE BEGINNING OF THE FULFILLMENT OF YOUR DREAM SEED.

The Master Key of
FAITH

Principle: Faith is the ability to believe
that something exists which
you do not presently see.

The Master Key of Faith

I know you are more excited than ever about your DREAM SEED.

Yes, your *marriage* can be *restored*. Your *body* can be completed *healed*. Yes, God can provide the *extra finances* you desperately need at this time.

And it can begin happening this very moment as you learn to use the most explosive weapon God has given you: YOUR FAITH.

Faith is that invisible confidence that something exists other than what you presently see. It is that internal belief system planted by God in every human being. Faith is the *ability to believe.*

THE "D.A.G."

Faith always draws the attention of God.

That's why I call it the "D.A.G." – the Divine Attention-Getter!

Just as repentance draws God's attention, so FAITH ALWAYS STIMULATES INCREDIBLE FAVOR FROM GOD AND HIS ANGELS. Yes, faith is the magnet that attracts God toward you. You don't have to drive a Rolls Royce to impress Him. Nor is it necessary to be a Harvard graduate.

God is impressed when you *use* the faith He has *already given you.*

"God hath dealt to every man the measure of faith" (Romans 12:3b).

"But without faith it is impossible to please him: for he that cometh to God must believe that he is, and that he is a rewarder of them that diligently seek him" (Hebrews 11:6).

Every miracle you receive can be traced to a SEED OF FAITH.

Faith is what drives ordinary men to accomplish the *extraordinary.*

Faith is what turns common men into *uncommon achievers.*

They possess different personalities and talents. *But they learned to use their faith.* They focused their believing toward their DREAM SEED.

Faith is the real difference between champions and losers.

Faith is the magic ingredient of every miracle.

It can cause your blind eyes to *see.*

It can cause your deaf ears to *hea*r again.

It can cause your lame legs to receive *strength.*

It can make your barren womb *productive.*

It can *heal* your scarred and empty marriage.

It can *restore confidence* into your broken heart.

It can *break the chains* of your cocaine habit or any drug addiction.

It can *change you* from an alcoholic into a great achiever again.

It can *transform* you from a weakling into the champion God intended you to be.

WHAT IS FAITH?

Few people can really explain faith. It is like electricity or the wind. You cannot hold it in your hand. You cannot seal it in a jar at your house, or package it like a box of corn flakes.

Yet, *faith is a substance.* God used it to create the universe.

"Through faith we understand that the worlds were framed by the word of God, so that things which are seen were not made of things which do appear" (Hebrews 11:30).

Faith is the *ability to believe.* Remember, it is the invisible confidence within you that something exists other than what you presently see.

The *proof* of your faith is revealed in your *pursuit of the unseen.*

Faith is a seed planted in the soil of your spirit. God planted it there at your birth. It is invisible to the natural eye, like minerals in the water. Yet it is very tangible in the realm of the spirit.

It may be *dead* or *dormant* – or *alive* and *growing.*

Faith that is *inactive* toward God is what we call DEAD FAITH. *"faith without works is dead" (James* 2:26b). The Bible also refers to it as "unbelief" or "doubt." It does not mean that a man is not using his faith. Rather, it means that he is not using his faith *productively*, or *toward God.* He may even be using it *against* himself in a destructive manner.

ACTIVE faith is when a man uses his believing ability to obtain something he wants from God. He usually will DO something to prove that he has confidence in the Word of God.

The starving widow in 1 Kings 17 willingly *gave her last meal* to the prophet Elijah. Naaman, the leper, obeyed the prophet and *dipped in the Jordan* River seven times.

At the wedding in Cana, they *filled up the water pots* in anticipation of the water-to-wine miracle. Noah, though he had never seen rain, *began to build the ark* in faith.

The presence of your faith is proven by something you do in obedience to God and His Word.

The ABILITY TO BELIEVE *already exists within you.* It's the substance called FAITH. Your faith is like a muscle. The more you use it, the stronger it will become.

I want to help you begin USING your faith to obtain the miracles and blessings God wants you to receive.

WHAT DOES THE BIBLE TEACH US ABOUT FAITH?

1. YOUR FAITH IS AN INVISIBLE SUBSTANCE.
   Like the wind or electricity, you may not see it with your natural eye, but its presence and force is proven by its results in your life. *"Now faith is the substance of things hoped for, the evidence of things not seen"* (Hebrews 11:1).

2. YOU ALREADY POSSESS THE SEED OF FAITH
   WITHIN YOU.
      BELIEVING ABILITY is within *every* person. You
   choose *how* you will use it. Whatever you choose to believe
   decides whether it will be *productive* or *destructive* to your
   life. *"God hath dealt to every man the measure of faith"*
   (Romans 12:3b).

3. WHENEVER YOU USE YOUR FAITH, YOU PLEASE
   THE HEART OF GOD.
      Don't you appreciate it when others trust you? Don't
   you feel humiliated and a bit angry when they show *lack* of
   trust? Then you know how God feels about your faith in
   Him! *"But without faith it is impossible to please him: for he
   that cometh to God must believe that he is, and that he is a
   rewarder of them that diligently seek him"* (Hebrews 11:6).

   Faith is very important to God.

   Please don't take this lightly. Sometimes we make
   statements such as, "Well, I just don't have much faith."
   How would you like to hear your children talking to their
   little friends, "Well, my mother and dad lie to me all the
   time. I just don't believe anything they say." You would
   be crushed, insulted and humiliated.

   Well, it is even more important that you trust the Word
   of God. God wants you to believe *every word* He speaks to
   you. You insult Him when you don't.

   When you *use* your faith, you are pleasing to God.

   When you don't trust Him, you disappoint God.

   It's just that simple.

I know several great men of God who are not necessarily perfect. They have made mistakes. But the principal secret of their success is that *they have learned to use their faith in God.*

4. YOU WILL CHANGE YOUR CIRCUMSTANCES WHEN YOU CHANGE THE DIRECTION OF YOUR BELIEVING.

   "if thou canst believe, all things are possible to him that believeth" (Mark 9:23).

   You will inevitably experience what you consistently expect.

   I believe it was Henry Ford who said that men who believe they *can* do something, and those who believe they *cannot*, are BOTH right.

   God really wants you healed. Dare to BELIEVE IT.

   God really wants you happy. Dare to BELIEVE IT.

   God really wants to supply all your needs. Dare to BELIEVE IT.

   One of my songs on a recent album is "Dare to Believe."

   "Dare to believe, and even demons tremble.
   Dare to believe, and sickness must depart.

   "Dare to believe, and even mountains can
   be cast into the sea.

   "Your world can change my friend, when
   you dare to believe."

"The seeds you have planted are not wasted.
They are ready to burst forth with new life.

"So today, my friend, let your faith be awakened.
Dare to believe that God is still alive!"

5. YOUR BIGGEST MOUNTAIN WILL SUCCUMB TO
YOUR SMALLEST SEED OF FAITH.
    *"If ye have faith as a grain of mustard seed, ye shall
say unto this mountain, Remove hence to yonder place;
and it shall remove; and nothing shall be impossible unto
you"* (Matthew 17:20b).

    You may feel as though you have little faith. I've felt
that way before, too. But Jesus did not say, "If you have
faith like a *mountain* you can move a *mustard seed!"* He said
that *your smallest act of faith is enough to get a mountain moved.*

    But you must ACT on your faith. You must *SPEAK* to
the mountain. YOU MUST TELL YOUR MOUNTAIN
EXACTLY WHAT YOU WANT IT TO DO. Sometimes,
you must *keep on* speaking to your mountain when it refuses
to budge. But when you learn this secret, the mountains in
your life WILL move. Jesus said it. *Believe it* and it will
start working for you.

6. YOU MUST PURSUE WHAT YOU REALLY BELIEVE
GOD WANTS YOU TO POSSESS.
    *"If any of you lack wisdom, let him ask of God, that
giveth to all men liberally, and upbraideth not; and it shall
be given him.
    But let him ask in faith, nothing wavering. For he that
wavereth is like a wave of the sea driven with the wind and
tossed"* (James 1:5,6).

Remember the earlier principle of desire: *The proof of desire is pursuit.* Miracles don't just happen where they are needed. They happen where they are *wanted.* Jesus did not always go where He was needed, but where He was *wanted.*

We rarely reach for the things we really need.

But we *always* reach for those things we truly *desire.*

7. YOUR GUARANTEE OF ETERNAL LIFE HINGES UPON YOUR FAITH IN JESUS CHRIST.
   "For God so loved the world, that he gave his only begotten Son, that whosoever believeth in him should not perish, but have everlasting life" (John 3:16).

I think we all have a built-in craving for immortality. In other words, we'd love to live *forever!*

The Bible clearly teaches there is life beyond the grave.

"Let not your heart be troubled: ye believe in God, believe also in me. In my Father's house are many mansions: if it were not so, I would have told you. I go to prepare a place for you. And if I go and prepare a place for you, I will come again, and receive you unto myself; that where I am, there ye may be also" (John 14:1-3).

I have never regretted my decision to accept Jesus Christ as my Lord and Savior. In fact, I wrote a song recently expressing my feelings about it.

"I wouldn't want to try to live
    without the Lord in my life.

"I wouldn't want to have to live
    in darkness when there is light.

"And I won't trade away
the joy I know today.

"I wouldn't want to try to live
without the Lord in my life."

Every man has a *"built-in believer"* within him.

What you choose to do with that *"believer"* decides your *present* happiness and even your ETERNAL FUTURE.

HOW TO INCREASE YOUR FAITH

Your faith is like a seed.

And like any seed, it must be *watered* and *nurtured* for it to grow. As the apostles said unto the Lord, *"Increase our faith"* (Luke 17:5b).

1. THE MOST IMPORTANT SECRET IN
   INCREASING YOUR FAITH IS TO HEAR
   THE SPOKEN WORD OF GOD.
   "So then faith cometh by hearing, and hearing by the word of God" (Romans 10:17).

   Do you own a cassette tape recorder? Then *use it.* Keep it plugged in for continuous use. Keep a stack of Scripture and teaching tapes close by.

   While you are shaving or bathing, *play those tapes.*

   While you are getting dressed, *play those tapes.*

   While you are waiting for your wife to get dressed, *play those tapes.*

While you are driving your car to work, *play those tapes*.

I usually keep tape recorders in every room of my house. And since I travel over 15,000 miles a month, I keep a tape deck in my motel room at all times. *Cassette tapes can feed your spirit.*

"Oh, but tapes cost too much," a little lady told me.

"Ignorance will cost you *more*," I replied.

It is amazing how we will pay $40 for a tank of gas that is gone in three days, while excusing ourselves from the purchasing of powerful, life-changing knowledge that could revolutionize our entire lifestyle.

Some people spend more money on their cars than they do their minds. *(Maybe that's why their cars run better than their minds!)*

Meditate on Scripture.

Memorize Scripture.

Talk about Scripture.

Compose songs with Scriptures.

2. BE HONEST WITH GOD ABOUT YOUR PERSONAL NEEDS AND DESIRES.
    "He that covereth his sins shall not prosper: but whoso confesseth and forsaketh them shall have mercy" (Proverbs 28:13).

"him that cometh to Me I will in no wise cast out" (John 6:37b).

It was a marvelous moment in my life when I learned to *speak* my real feelings *aloud* to God. I discovered that He would never ask me to do something that I could not do. He would not ask me to achieve something I could not accomplish.

You see, I hate to make mistakes. I really do. Any kind of mistake. Whether it is getting lost on a strange freeway or failing to spot a mis-spelled word in my current newsletter! And Satan delights in taking advantage of that kind of conscientiousness.

He wants us to feel that we are incapable of pleasing God. I've had moments when I felt that God was simply unfair. I felt that His standard was just too high for anyone to achieve – especially me!

It is not always easy to live holy.

I sometimes have difficulty understanding the head-in-the-clouds, glib-tongued Christian who says that he never experiences adversity. Personally, I have found that the same thing happened in the lives of Joseph, Daniel and the Apostle Paul.

Is it humanly possible for us to please God? *Yes, without a doubt.*

Do you really *want* to live in obedience? Then *tell Him.* He needs to hear it from your own lips.

I've found that God is the easiest person to please that I have ever known. He is *consistent* in His expectations, incredibly longsuffering and unwavering in His confidence in me.

The real truth is that people are harder to please than God! Subconsciously, each of us attempts to please those around us. It is impossible. *Therein is the weariness of life.*

MAN-PLEASING IS ENSLAVING. As Proverbs 29:25 says, *"The fear of man bringeth a snare: but whoso putteth his trust in the LORD shall be safe."*

I've found that one of the keys to pleasing God is to focus ONLY on *24-hour achievements.* This simply means to discern *each morning* what will make Him happy for that day *only.* Then CONCENTRATE on His goals for *just that day.*

3. VERBALLY EXPRESS THE PRESENCE OF GOD THAT IS NOW WITHIN YOU.
As a believer, you already contain the power of God within you. *Release it!* Don't bottle it up. Uncork it!

"He that believeth on Me, as the scripture hath said, out of his belly shall flow rivers of living water" (John 7:38).

Don't let anyone clog up that inner river inside you. Someone near you today desperately needs the Water of Life from *your* well!

Feel Jesus. *Think* Jesus. *Talk* about Jesus!

Don't hesitate to pray for someone on the street or in a restaurant. The *whole* world is *your* turf. *Dominate it!*

HEALING THE SICK IS MORE IMPORTANT
THAN ACCOMMODATING A CRITIC.

WHAT HAPPENS WHEN YOU "DOMINATE YOUR TURF"?

You will *neutralize* your adversaries.

You will *nullify* Satanic strategy being planned against you.

And most important of all, you will be DOING THE WORKS OF JESUS.

"The Spirit of the Lord is upon me, because he hath anointed me to preach the gospel to the poor; he hath sent me to heal the brokenhearted, to preach deliverance to the captives, and recovering of sight to the blind, to set at liberty them that are bruised, to preach the acceptable year of the Lord" (Luke 4:18,19).

Several key suggestions:

- AVOID TRIVIAL CONVERSATIONS
  THAT MAY ENCOURAGE
  SLANDEROUS WORDS OR STRIFE.

  "Be not deceived: evil communications corrupt good manners" (1 Corinthians 15:33). Remember, you are like a well of water. Don't allow others to dump their trash into the well of your spirit.

- SANCTIFY A PRIVATE PLACE
  FOR DAILY PRAYER.

  It may be in your bedroom, bathroom or even outdoors. It is good to have a *special place* to fellowship with God.

Learn to meditate *alone*. God will not scream His instructions. Your ability to *hear* is *His* gift to you. Your ability to *listen* is *your* gift to Him. *"He that hath an ear, let him hear what the Spirit saith"* (Revelation 3:6a).

- ### LEARN TO RECOGNIZE THE IMMEDIATE AND CONSTANT PRESENCE OF GOD.

  "...he that cometh to God must believe that he is..." (Hebrews 11:6). God is not a million miles away from you. He is here! Right now, even while you are reading these very words.

  "The LORD is nigh unto all them that call upon him, to all that call upon him in truth" (Psalm 145:18).

  "When thou passest through the waters, I will be with thee; and through the rivers, they shall not overflow thee: when thou walkest through the fire, thou shalt not be burned; neither shall the flame kindle upon thee" (Isaiah 43:2).

  Your problems don't scare God! He was defeating Satan before you were even born! He is with you NOW, *even at your lowest point of need.*

- ### ESTABLISH A REGULAR FASTING SCHEDULE.

  Don't fast only when you "feel like it." Decide *specific* days or meals that you will fast and get alone with God. Some will complain of legalism and bondage. Some may be unable to because of health reasons. (I suggest that you consult your physician about any fasting you decide to do.)

Fasting has dramatically changed my life. Whether long 21-day fasts, or a simple one-day fast, I've experienced *revelation of truth, financial ideas* and *unusual power* to carry out commands from God. Also, I have found that my *fear of opposition and criticism completely shrivels* on an extended fast. It seems that my *self-confidence multiplies* and completely displaces any fear of men who might oppose me.

Without a doubt, *my faith seems to increase* every time I fast and seek God. *"Howbeit this kind goeth not out but by prayer and fasting"* (Matthew 17:21).

- CONSTANTLY PICTURE THE REWARDS THAT YOUR DREAM SEED WILL PRODUCE.

I'll never forget my first car. It was a black, 1953 Chevrolet Coupe. Although the car was worth about $225, the seller insisted on $300. I was just 18 years old, and $300 was mighty big money for a high school kid in those days.

I was a bit upset with the price tag, but several things kept surfacing that were more important than the money. First, the owner appeared trustworthy and had kept the car in top running condition. Second, it was a low-mileage car and the best deal I had been able to locate.

And third, I really *needed* the car to maintain a good job I had at a local food store.

The more I concentrated on the *benefits* of the car, the less important the cost became to me. I *pictured* myself sitting behind the wheel. I could almost breathe the air of *freedom* it gave me!

The more I pictured the REWARDS of ownership, the more excited I became about that car. I bought it. I loved it. And I was able to enjoy it for several good years.

You see, my *picturing* the benefits of the car *increased my desire for it.*

Would you like to do something GOOD for yourself today?

Then, start *picturing miracles.*

Start *picturing your healing.*

Start *picturing your marriage coming together.*

Start *picturing your bills completely paid.*

It is a Master Secret that will INCREASE YOUR FAITH.

Abraham pictured his children. (Romans 4:18-21.)

Joseph pictured himself in a palace. (Genesis 37:5-9.)

Jesus pictured His resurrection. (Hebrews 12:2.)

Remember, *your life will always move in the direction of your DOMINANT thought.*

IT IS THE GOLDEN SECRET OF GREAT FAITH.

A SPECIAL WORD TO THOSE
TROUBLED BY UNBELIEF

Please read this carefully. I experienced great doubts during crisis points earlier in my life. Over a two-year period I fought waves of doubt regarding the infallibility of the Scriptures. And it seemed that no one could answer my questions to my satisfaction. It appeared to me that there were contradictions in the Word of God. I prayed sincere prayers that seemed to go unanswered.

Yet, deep within me I longed to believe – in God, in miracles and in the validity of the Scriptures.

So I finally prayed this prayer, "God if you really do exist, you must be capable of giving me the dynamic faith I need to become a true believer. Please do it."

It happened. Gradually, truth began to fit like pieces in a puzzle. And with each piece came a measure of *peace.*

Slowly, my inner storm began to subside. Today, I can hardly believe I ever doubted His existence.

You see, this is what I had to face: Whether you are an atheist who believes in evolution, or a Christian who believes in the Genesis account of creation, *you WILL always believe in something.*

Either way, *I had to do something with the faith inside of me.*

THE EVIDENCE OF HIS PRESENCE FAR OUTWEIGHED THE PROOF OF HIS ABSENCE.

I chose to believe. I have never, for a single moment, regretted it.

Let me explain that UNBELIEF is not necessarily a lack of faith. You see, *all men have the ability to believe.* Believing is the invisible confidence that something exists other than what you presently see.

Unbelief is really *misdirected* and *misused* faith. It is believing the opinions of men, instead of the opinions of God.

The Israelites in the Old Testament are an example. They sent 12 men to spy out Canaan, the Promised Land. Ten returned with a report of *defeat.* They said that the giants were too strong for Israel to overcome.

However, two spies, Joshua and Caleb, brought a report of *victory.* They *acknowledged* that the giants existed, but *chose to believe the promise of God* that they could possess the land.

Did the 10 spies have faith? Certainly. Their faith was in the *ability of the giants* INSTEAD OF *the ability of God.*

Remember that *faith is believing that something exists that you have not yet experienced.* The giants had not yet defeated them. Yet they chose to believe in their own *unseen* and *unexperienced defeat.*

Again, I emphasize that this misuse of faith is what is commonly called *doubt,* or unbelief. It is deadly and destructive. It will destroy you and kill every dream God has ever planted within you.

I urge you to *confront* and *resist* the spirit of unbelief that assaults you today. And in Jesus' name, start using your God-given faith to move the mountains in your life.

You can do it. And, you can do it TODAY.

"MY PRECIOUS FATHER, I come boldly to you today in the name of Jesus. I come in behalf of my friend who is reading this book in desperate need of miracles in his life.

"You gave him his DREAM SEED of his Desired Miracle and Blessing, and You will not let him fail.

"I BIND the spirit of unbelief and doubt that has invaded his *mind*, his *home* and his *heart*. I COMMAND every demon spirit to come out and depart from his life. I LOOSE him and set him free in the name of Jesus of Nazareth. I FORBID those spirits to ever return into his life again."

Now my friend, I RELEASE the presence of Jesus *into your life*. Receive the forgiveness and healing power of Jesus Christ *into your mind*, your *heart*, your *body* and your *soul*.

Be healed in your *mind*.

Be healed in your *emotions*.

Be healed in your *memories*.

Be healed in your *body*.

Be healed in your *marriage*.

Be healed in your *finances*.

Be healed of your *broken heart*.

Be healed of *alcoholism*.

Be healed of *drug addiction*.

Be healed of your *inferiority complex.*

Be healed of your *sense of unworthiness.*

Be healed of your *lack of confidence.*

"I pray this today in the powerful and precious NAME OF JESUS OF NAZARETH, Who loves you and gave His life for your *complete deliverance* and TOTAL FREEDOM.

"In Jesus' name, IT IS DONE. Amen."

The Master Key of
SEED-FAITH

Principle: When something leaves your
hand toward God, something
leaves God's hand toward you.

The Master Key of Seed-Faith

It was a golden day in my life when I discovered that *I could give away something I possessed* – A SEED – *to receive something that I did not presently possess* – A HARVEST.

A seed is *anything you can contribute to another.* It is anything you are capable of giving away! An *hour of your time* invested in someone with a need, is a *seed. Kind words...friendships... loyalty...money...anything* that you plant toward people or God's work is what is called A SEED.

SEED-FAITH is when you plant your seed with EXPECTATION of a specific harvest. It is your seed – planted IN FAITH for a SPECIFIC RESULT OR MIRACLE.

God planted His best seed – JESUS – to create a harvest: THE FAMILY OF GOD. He *gave* something He treasured to reap an even *greater benefit.* His DREAM SEED was the Body of Christ, His Church. His *seed* was His Son, Jesus Christ.

This is the principle of SEED-FAITH. It is the opposite of selfishness that operates in the world system. Selfishness is *hoarding;* selfishness is *depriving another to your own advantage. Seed-faith is giving away something you have, to create something you don't have.*

This is how I learned the importance of my gifts and offerings to God. When I give an offering to God – *my money* – I am giving Him a part of me – my time, my skills, my energy, my labor. *My money represents me.* This explains Proverbs 3:9,10.

"Honour the LORD with thy substance, and with the firstfruits of all thine increase: So shall thy barns be filled with plenty, and thy presses shall burst out with new wine." Seed-faith is the golden thread in 1 Kings 17 that explains the miracle of supply for the widow woman in the famine. She *gave* to Elijah, the man of God, *something that she possessed* – A SEED – to *receive something she did not presently possess* – A FOOD SUPPLY. She sowed her seed in EXPECTATION *after* the prophet explained the seed-faith principle of EXPECTING *a desired result.*

Most people do not understand this; certainly our logic tells us that our giving will only diminish our supply. Therein is the power of seed-faith. *Our Offerings are proof of our believing* – that something exists though we do not presently see it.

I cannot overemphasize how the principle of seed-faith has changed my life.

DRASTICALLY.

And I'm grateful for remarkable men of God, like Oral Roberts, who have the patience to help us understand it.

You see, when I walked out of the Texas courtroom, I felt utterly hopeless. I could scarcely afford to purchase even a sofa for my small, one-bedroom apartment. Many nights I sat alone, drained and confused, even questioning the validity of this "Gospel of Prosperity," as some have called it.

That's when I decided to test the Scriptures myself. Malachi 3 was an open invitation from God to "prove His very existence and in particular the principle of prosperity through *giving.*

Nearly everyone believes in financial increase. Our credit cards prove that we even plan for it! Nearly everyone believes they deserve more than they are getting in life. But only in recent years are many of us beginning to grasp that SEED-FAITH GIVING is one of the Master Keys to the miracles we need.

It seems to be happening everywhere. I receive letters every day from friends and partners who are ecstatic over the results of their practicing the principle of seed-faith. I am constantly amazed at the flow of miracles into my own life through my learning this principle.

I must be honest with you. The principle of seed-faith was very difficult for me to accept at first. I really struggled with it. At times, I felt that it was just another method used by some ministers to raise funds for their ministries.

I understood tithing, the giving of 10 percent of my total income back to God. I had been taught that principle since childhood, and I practiced it faithfully.

I just didn't understand giving something to God and expecting to receive a miracle in return for it. It seemed to be a very cheap, selfish motive for giving to God. I equated it with "buying a miracle."

Once, I even declared publicly, "When I give to God, I expect nothing in return." That seemed to make me feel more pure, more spiritual, more unselfish.

Somehow, the idea that there might even be a difference between tithing and giving never really dawned on me.

Though I was a tither, SOMETHING WAS MISSING. And deep inside, I knew it. Oh, God blessed me in many ways. And I don't doubt that my tithing played a great part. But I knew deep inside that God wanted me to experience much more. He wanted to reveal secrets I had not yet discovered.

Little did I know that I was standing on the threshold of a Niagara Falls of miracles and blessings.

I had studied the tithing system in the Scriptures. Abraham was the first man in the Bible to practice it. *"And he gave him tithes of all"* (Genesis 14:20b).

His son, Issac, and his grandson, Jacob, tithed also. As I said in an earlier chapter, Jesus, in the New Testament, even commended the Pharisees for practicing tithing. *"...ye pay tithe of mint and anise and cummin, and have omitted the weightier matters of the law, judgment, mercy, and faith: these ought ye to have done, and not to leave the other undone"* (Matthew 23:23).

WHAT IS TITHING?

Tithing is *returning* to God the 10 percent of your total income which He personally designated for Himself. (The word *tithe* means "tenth.")

"And all the tithe of the land, whether of the seed of the land, or of the fruit of the tree, is the LORD's: it is holy unto the LORD. And concerning the tithe of the herd, or of the flock, even of whatsoever passeth under the rod, the tenth shall be holy unto the LORD" (Leviticus 27:30,32).

Some people feel that these Scriptures applied to the old Testament Israelites only. However, I think a little further study proves otherwise.

First, Abraham gave tithe BEFORE the Law was given to Moses. (Genesis 14:20.)

Second, Jesus recognized it as a worthwhile practice even among the unworthy Pharisees. (Matthew 23:23.) Third, if it was meant for the seed of Abraham, that includes those in Christ.

"And if ye be Christ's, then are ye Abraham's seed, and heirs according to the promise" (Galatians 3:29). Fourth, there is no Scripture that refutes tithing to render it an obsolete practice.

WHO SHOULD RECEIVE YOUR TITHE?

Opinions differ as to whom our tithe should be given.

Some believe it should be given to the poor, or to their parents or other worthwhile causes. Actually, what we give to the poor and needy is called "alms." Your tithe, however, is different. Remember, *the tithe belongs to the Lord*. It does not really belong to you. It belongs to the Lord and His work – actually to those in the ministry. Ephesians 4:11 states: *"And He gave some, apostles; and some, prophets; and some, evangelists; and some, pastors and teachers."*

It appears that in the Scriptures the tithe was received by the priesthood of Israel, or those in spiritual leadership. It was their major means of support. *"And behold, I have given the children of Levi [the priesthood] all the tenth in Israel for an inheritance, for their service which they serve, even the service of the tabernacle of the congregation"* (Numbers 18:21).

Another helpful insight is given in Malachi 3:10, *"Bring ye all the tithes into the storehouse, that there may be meat in mine house..."* We are to financially support those from who we draw our primary spiritual knowledge and encouragement.

Let's review for a moment. *The Lord's tithe is a tenth of your total income.* It doesn't really belong to you at all. *It belongs to God.* You are simply responsible for RETURNING His ten percent back into His work for the continuation of the Gospel.

GOD'S REACTION TO A NON-TITHER

God guarantees supernatural, abundant supply back into the life of a tither. *"Bring ye all the tithes into the storehouse, that there may be meat in mine house, and prove me now herewith, saith the LORD of hosts, if I will not open you the windows of heaven, and pour you out a blessing, that there shall not be room enough to receive it.*

"And I will rebuke the devourer for your sakes, and he shall not destroy the fruits of your ground; neither shall your vine cast her fruit before the time in the field, saith the LORD of hosts" (Malachi 3:10,11).

After a service one night in Houston, Texas, a young couple approached me for special prayer.

"Brother Mike, we are really having a financial struggle," they confided. "Unless God gives us a miracle, we will lose everything we own."

As I reached for their hands to join in the prayer of agreement, something inside my spirit stopped me. I felt impressed to ask them a question.

"Do you tithe regularly?" I asked.

"Well, no," the young wife said rather reluctantly.

"We can't afford to tithe right now," her husband added somewhat defensively. "When we make more money, we intend to start paying it then."

I knew the subject was sensitive, but I had to tell them the truth.

"It really won't help for me to pray for your financial situation," I explained. "Whether you realize it or not, *you are stealing from God.* The tithe is not yours to spend on yourself. I believe it is wrong for you to even pay personal bills with it."

They were crestfallen. Evidently, they had never taken the tithe that seriously.

I explained that the tithe was *holy.* I explained that they had *misused* holy money. *They had stolen something that belonged to the Lord and sowed it back into themselves.* This could very well explain their financial curse.

The Apostle Paul painted a shocking portrait in Galatians 6:6-10. He said that we are to *sow seeds into the lives of spiritual teachers.* However, when we take those holy seeds and sow them back into our own lives *instead,* we "shall of the flesh reap corruption."

I believe thousands are creating misfortunes and even tragedies in their own lives because of their resentment and rebellion to God's command to support ministers of the Gospel.

DON'T KEEP SOMETHING THAT BELONGS TO THE LORD.

I've seen champion men and women plummet to failure because they became greedy. Some become angry at their pastor or an evangelist and retaliated by withholding their tithes and offerings.

These ministers may suffer temporarily; *but the non-givers have sown seed to their own destruction.* The harvest of our disobedience is simply not worth our withholding the Lord's tithe.

MY GOLDEN DISCOVERY — SEED-FAITH GIVING

It hit me like a bolt of lightning one day....

The Scriptures said that Israel had robbed God in the tithe AND OFFERINGS. Was there really a difference?

I can't explain it. But somehow I knew there was a dimension of blessings beyond the act of tithing. There was a reason why some Christians barely made it financially each month, while others were prospering. That's when I discovered the difference between the act of TITHING and the attitude of GIVING.

The tithe *already* belongs to God. It is a predesignated ten percent established as a beginning practice in my financial partnership with God. It is not an option or a matter of choice.

Let's suppose I use your car for a few days. I bring it back to your house Sunday morning with this statement: "Hi, John. I have a special gift for you today. I want to donate this car to you and your wife!"

How would you feel? You'd laugh, wouldn't you? Of course. You see, the car is not an optional gift because it already *belonged* to you. But suppose I purchased new tires while I was using your car as a gesture of gratitude. The tires were optional. I chose to give them to you in addition to the car. This is the basic difference between our tithe and our offerings. Our tithes and offerings are SEEDS THAT WE PLANT TOWARD A DESIRED FUTURE HARVEST.

Tithing is the act of *returning* the ten percent portion of TODAY'S salary. It is by acknowledgment and recognition of

God as the Owner and Possessor of all things. (Genesis 14:19,20.) My offerings are the optional amount that I give above my tithe. *Giving is the attitude that I am replanting* the large tithe and my offerings as a *seed* toward tomorrow's supply.

Something happened in my spirit when I saw this picture. My tithing is my act of *obedience*. My offerings are optional *investments* above the tithe. *My seed-faith giving is planting my tithes and offerings with expectation of a specific desired harvest.*

My attitude began to change about the whole idea of giving. In the early years, I felt like the tithe was a debt, an obligation, a burden. It made me cling to the 90 percent as if I had to make up for the ten percent I had lost to God!

But suddenly I realized that *God wanted to be my business partner.* He wanted to help me succeed. The ten percent that I returned each month to Him established my *foundation* for financial success. My offerings to Him became my extra *seeds* REPLANTED toward my *future* supply.

Now, some theologians might disagree. But I refuse to argue about what I know has worked for me. I know that miracles and blessings have poured into my life since I began practicing the principle of seed-faith.

MY PERSONAL MIRACLE SUPPLY

I don't think I'll ever forget it as long as I live. Some years ago I was conducting services at a Christian retreat. It was my turn to speak and conclude the evening service. As I was receiving the offering at the close, I suddenly felt an intense urge to give $1,000!

I was momentarily stunned. You see, I had always been a "$100-man." (Everyone has an A.L.G. – an Average Level of Giving. Some give $5, others will regularly give $20. So I usually felt pretty generous when I wrote out my check for $100!)

Well, I didn't immediately respond to that urge. After all, I reasoned, there's a whole stack of bills coming due. I can't afford to write out a check every time I get a little emotional and generous.

I kept waiting, and that small, Inner Voice kept whispering, "$1,000." "But I've never given $1,000 before in my life," I argued with myself. *"And that means that you have never reaped the harvest from a $1,000 seed before, either,"* responded the Inner Voice.

Well, I was quite desperate to raise my A.L.R. – my Average Level of Receiving! And I knew that it would never happen until I upgraded my A.L.G.!

I think I shocked my secretary when I called the next day.

"Please write a check for $1,000 and send it to me."

I wish space permitted details of what began to happen.

Within 15 days, a partner walked into my office with a seed-faith offering of $10,000 – the largest offering I'd ever received in my entire ministry at that time. Several days later, I opened an envelope from a partner in Houston, Texas. "Mike, God spoke to my heart to plant a seed of $10,000 into your ministry."

The miracles had begun.

Some months later, I moved from California to Dallas, Texas, to be more centralized for crusade travel. God made it possible for me to buy a home, but I didn't have enough money to buy furniture.

Then a royalty check of almost $5,000 arrived. I was elated. At last I would be able to purchase some furnishings for my new home.

Soon after, a well-known evangelist asked me to spend five weeks co-hosting his daily television program. At that time, he was asking partners to join the Hall of Faith with a special one-time offering of $1,000.

You guessed it.

As I spoke on seed-faith giving, I felt an inner urge. "Take $1,000 from your 'furnishings fund' and join the Hall of Faith."

After a few minutes of ignoring the prompting of the Holy Spirit, I finally said, "I feel impressed of the Lord to plant a seed of $1,000 today." Though I felt a little awkward, I knew in my heart that I had done the right thing.

The second day came. The scene was the same. He exhorted the partners again to plant an additional seed of $1,000 for a loved one who was very special in their lives. I immediately thought of my son, Jason.

And, again, I felt what was becoming a familiar feeling, that inner urge to plant another seed-faith offering of $1,000. I did.

That afternoon was quite emotional for me. My heart was at peace. But my mind was whirling. *Had I acted impulsively?*

Was my giving really prompted by God, or had I merely been caught up in the momentum of the telethon?

Let me insert a brief word. I have since learned that God will compensate even for impulsive giving when we do it with a pure desire to be obedient. You may make a mistake or two in your giving. But it won't be fatal. The most important thing is to develop that *instant responsiveness* to the promptings of the Holy Spirit.

By this time the money I had earmarked for house furnishings had dwindled to $3,000. Hardly adequate to properly furnish a large, empty house!

I flew to Dallas for a scheduled speaking engagement. The church was young and vibrant, and running about 300 in attendance. When I got up to speak, the public address system began to squawk and screech. Turning to the pastor I shook my head.

"You folks need a new P.A. system here," I said, somewhat unnecessarily.

Embarrassed, he replied, "Yes, I know."

"Why don't you buy a new one?" I asked. (It always amazes me that we will spend millions of dollars on buildings and then buy a bargain-basement microphone over which we preach the unsearchable riches of Christ. I still believe that the work of God deserves the best equipment available! However, this was not the case with my pastor friend. They were simply having some financial struggles.)

"Mike, we just don't have enough money," he explained.

"How much to you need?"

"It would take $4,000 or more to purchase what we really need," he replied.

Almost before I could think, it just popped out of my mouth.

"I'll give the first $1,000 if 30 of your people will stand right now and give $100 each for a new P.A. system," I said, turning to the congregation.

Their response was overwhelming. More than 30 members stood almost instantly. And I was happy for them. God had used me to motivate their faith.

There was just one small problem. *My house furnishing fund was now down to $2,000!* Believe me, I had a real talk with God that afternoon! I had such mixed emotions. I've always prided myself on being a man of logic. And there is always a need for planning and thinking ahead. But something unusual and extraordinary was happening. I just needed reassurance from Him.

I learned one of my greatest lessons from God that day.

He showed me the difference between logic and faith.

Logic will *analyze.*

Faith will *ACT.*

Logic demands an *explanation.*

Faith merely needs *motivation.*

Logic rarely produces miracles. Faith *always* produces miracles.

Logic plans around things that are visible. *Faith plans on things that are invisible.*

I remember that afternoon like it was yesterday. The presence of God was so warm and precious. "Son, I respect a man who doesn't try to negotiate with Me. I asked you to plant that seed for a reason. *When I get ready to give you a harvest, I will always ask you for a seed to unlock that harvest.*"

My heart was brimming with anticipation. God touched me with an unusual anointing during the evening service. Afterwards, a middle-aged man approached me.

"Mike, I own a rare sports car. In fact, there were only 19 of this particular model manufactured. Mine happens to be Serial No. 1. *God spoke to me to give it to you as a gift.*"

I was flabbergasted.

The following day, another miracle occurred. A businessman friend walked into my office. "Mike, I know you have been needing a van for your ministry. Go ahead and order it. *God told me to buy it for you.*"

I was astounded. It was almost too much, too fast.

The attitudes of people were changing toward me. It was incredible! I felt it in the air. It was as though favor was flowing toward me from every direction. There was an unusual aura around me that I could not explain. It was electrifying.

Then the principle became clear: WHAT I AM, I CREATE. Whatever I am, I will *reproduce* around me. *I am a seed.* My atmosphere is the harvest. WHAT I AM, I WILL CREATE AROUND ME.

I am of Irish decent. What will I create? Irishmen.

If you are a German, what do you create? Germans.

If you are a watermelon, what do you create? Watermelons.

If you are a giver, what do you create? GIVERS.

You see, my nature indirectly *affects*, and yes, even *controls* the nature of those around me.

This startled me. Was God actually giving me the power to unlock the giving of others toward me? The revelation was almost mind-boggling.

You see, Jesus did not say that God BECAME a Giver because I chose to BECOME a Giver. GOD HAS ALWAYS BEEN A GIVER.

Rather, He promised that *my giving would release a desire within men around me to give to me.* These men could be NEW ENTRY POINTS through which God, Who is my Source, could pour blessings into my life.

Two days later, a major ministry gave me *a check for $10,000!* It so happened that I had a bank loan due for that same amount – $10,000. Elated, I called my secretary to inform her that God had provided the full amount to pay off the loan. I would be placing it in the mail shortly. (Little did I know what was ahead!)

The scene again was the same television studio.

We had just gone off the air. Ralph Wilkerson, pastor of Melodyland in Anaheim, California, was asking for 50 new partners to give $1,000 to join the Hall of Faith. Strangely, almost no one moved forward.

Ralph suddenly turned to me and, thrusting the microphone in my hand said, "Mike, what is God speaking to you?"

"Uh, uh, nothing yet," I stuttered nervously. I asked everyone in the studio audience to bow their heads and pray.

Then I knew. Someone in that audience was supposed to sow a seed-faith offering of $10,000.

I immediately told the people what I felt.

"Someone is here today who should plant a seed of $10,000. I don't know your name. I just want to urge you to obey the voice of the Holy Spirit."

NOBODY MOVED.

I began to pray that God would give that person an obedient heart.

Suddenly, I felt a sickening sensation in the pit of my stomach. Surely it wasn't MY $10,000 that I had just received from another ministry! God knew I needed that to pay off the loan!

The inner nudging persisted. I knew I HAD to give that $10,000. (At the same time, I felt someone else was supposed to give $10,000, also.)

"If you obey God and give that $10,000 today, I will match it and give $10,000 also," I blurted out to the audience.

A lady lifted her hand and came forward.

And, there went my $10,000!

A friend asked me later if I felt good about giving it away.

"Hopeful is a better word!" I replied. I hear a lot of people talk about giving "cheerfully." Well, I know that God loves a cheerful giver, but it doesn't say that He hates an uncheerful one! Part of me felt good about giving the $10,000. Another part of me was a little worried. I had another long talk with the Lord that afternoon!

A great healing evangelist had told me once that miracles were constantly *coming toward* us or *passing us by*. I thought about this, and somehow knew that my instant response to the impressions of the Holy Spirit would draw the attention of God. My $10,000 seed, like a magnet, would now attract blessings I otherwise would not experience.

You see, *WHEN I LET GO OF SOMETHING IN MY HAND, GOD LETS GO OF SOMETHING IN HIS HAND FOR ME.* In fact, my friend Derek Floyd wrote a song on this very principle after I preached it.

Well, it happened.

The next day on the program, it was mentioned that I had given $10,000 the previous day. A lady in Birmingham, Alabama, was watching the program. As those words were spoken, the Holy Spirit spoke to her heart, "Replace Mike Murdock's $10,000 gift." That week I received her $10,000 seed-faith offering in the mail!

WHEN I RELEASED SOMETHING THAT WAS VISIBLE, GOD RELEASED SOMETHING THAT HAD BEEN INVISIBLE TO ME.

I wish I had the space to relate every miracle that I have experienced through instant response to the faith-pictures within me.

Some might regard this kind of giving as impulsive. But I know the voice of the Holy Spirit. And *I know how highly He regards obedience.*

I also believe that *our giving conquers greed.* And what is more important in the materialistic, money-grabbing world in which we live today?

THE NEW ORLEANS MIRACLE

I held a crusade in New Orleans, Louisiana. The pastor has been a personal, longtime friend. While I was in my teens, he motivated me tremendously to go to Bible college and to pursue the ministry. (As it happened, I had received another royalty check for slightly more than $10,000 the week before.)

Well, I have never made a practice of asking for a financial guarantee from the churches where I speak. Instead, I simply ask that an offering be received in each service for my ministry. And I always take a moment before the offering to explain the basic principles of giving.

It was Sunday night. I began to give my usual teaching on the Laws of Blessing prior to the offering.

As I spoke, the Holy Spirit began to instruct me. "Don't receive this offering for your own ministry. *Give the entire offering to their television ministry.*"

Well, my own ministry was in real need at this time. I felt that this offering was crucial. It's a peculiar thing: GOD HAS ALWAYS ASKED ME TO GIVE MY LARGEST SEED WHEN I WAS FACING MY GREATEST NEED.

I instinctively knew that God must be planning an unusual harvest to make such a demand on my faith. The more I thought about it, the more willing I became! So I told the people:

"God just spoke to my heart. This offering will not be for my own ministry after all. Instead, we are to plant our seeds tonight in the television ministry of your pastor."

Then I began to elaborate on the soul winning potential of television, quoting Proverbs 11:30, *"...he that winneth souls is wise."* I asked that each *focus their seed* toward the reaping of a *particular harvest* they were needing in their own lives.

Suddenly a picture of the royalty check I had just received flashed into my mind. Again, I heard the unmistakable voice of God. "I also want you to give the $10,000 you have just received in royalties."

I was sick inside. Really! I'm sure you can imagine my emotions – and my reaction! "Why, God? This is *two times in a row.* You didn't make Abraham try to kill Isaac *twice!"*

You would think by now I had learned that His reward would exceed my sacrifice. But I'm still human. There is still a part of me that sometimes wants to hoard and hold back.

It was one of the few times I seriously questioned God. Then He said something I shall never forget.

"Son, it is YOUR choice. I am giving you special faith to give $10,000 again. It may be one or two years before I ever give you this kind of faith again. CAN YOU WAIT THAT LONG FOR YOUR HARVEST?

I gave the $10,000.

The miracles began seven days later.

I received two phone calls that resulted in thousands of dollars of free television air time!

Oh, I thank God for His revelations, His promptings, His faithfulness.

"I have been young, and now am old; yet have I not seen the righteous forsaken, nor his seed begging bread" (Psalm 37:25).

Yes, the MASTER KEY of SEED-FAITH is still unlocking the DREAM SEEDS of those who will really *dare to believe it.*

My Closing Notes

This book is only a part of the whole picture in achieving your DREAM SEED. There are a few additional things I want to remind you of:

1. Your DREAM SEED must originate in the *heart of God* before its fulfillment will satisfy you.

2. You must *personally be persuaded* that it is from the heart of God.

3. You must be willing to *fight for* and *protect* your DREAM SEED from criticism and any Satanic substitutions.

4. You must *discern any distraction* to your DREAM SEED immediately and refuse its having any place in your life.

5. Your DREAM SEED must have time and attention to germinate and come into clear focus.

6. Your DREAM SEED must become the *dominant obsession* of your life, filling up every available space within you, crowding out every distraction and every adversary.

OVERCOMING THE ENEMIES OF YOUR DREAM SEED

Your DREAM SEED is like a rose in a garden of weeds. It will sometimes struggle to receive sunshine and water among the thorns of frustrated and unconcerned friends around you. *Never discuss your DREAM SEED carelessly.*

Avoid physical and emotional exhaustion. It will always blur your vision of your DREAM SEED. Your observations will become distorted and you will draw wrong conclusions. Remember, *conquering your doubts and critics* is an important part of achieving your DREAM SEED.

Like the guards placed around the bank vault, Satan always stations his forces *near* your miracle. So when your battle is the most difficult, that is usually an indication that *you are at the very scene of the fulfillment of your DREAM SEED.*

"And let us not be weary in well doing: for in due season we shall reap, if we faint not" (Galatians 6:9).

ABOUT MIKE MURDOCK

▶ Has embraced his assignment to pursue...possess...and publish the Wisdom of God to heal the broken in his generation.

▶ Preached his first public sermon at the age of 8.

▶ Preached his first evangelistic crusade at the age of 15.

▶ Began full-time evangelism at the age of 19, in which he has continued for 28 years.

▶ Has traveled and spoken to more than 11,000 audiences in 36 countries, including East Africa, the Orient, and Europe.

▶ Receives more than 1,500 invitation each year to speak in churches, colleges, and business corporations.

▶ Noted author of 57 books, including the best sellers, "Wisdom for Winning", "Dream-Seeds", and "The Double Diamond Principle".

▶ Created the popular "Wisdom Topical Bible" series for Businessmen, Mothers, Fathers, Teenagers, and the One-Minute Pocket Bible.

▶ Has composed more than 1,200 songs such as "I Am Blessed", "You Can Make It", and "Jesus Just The Mention of Your Name", recorded by many gospel artists.

▶ He has released over 20 music albums as well, and the music video, "Going Back To The Word".

▶ Is a dynamic teacher having produced to date 21 Wisdom Teaching Tape series and 9 School of Wisdom videos.

▶ He has appeared often on TBN, CBN, and other television network programs.

▶ Is a Founding Trustee on the Board of Charismatic Bible Ministries.

▶ Is the Founder of the Wisdom Training Center, for the training of those entering the ministry.

▶ Has had more than 3,400 accept the call into full-time ministry under his ministry.

▶ Has a goal of establishing Wisdom Rooms in one million Christian homes.

▶ Has a weekly television program called "Wisdom for Crisis Times".

MY DECISION PAGE

May I Invite You To Make Jesus The Lord of Your Life?

The Bible says,"that if thou shalt confess with thy mouth the Lord Jesus Christ, and shalt believe in thine heart that God hath raised him from the dead, thou shalt be saved. For with the heart man believeth unto righteousness; and with the mouth confession is made unto salvation." (Romans 10:9,10)

To receive Jesus Christ as Lord and Saviour of your life, please pray this prayer from your heart today!

Dear Jesus,
    I believe that You died for me and that You arose again on the third day. I confess to You that I am a sinner and that I need Your love and forgiveness. Come into my life, forgive my sins, and give me eternal life. I confess You now as my Saviour! I walk in your peace and joy from this day forward.

Signed _____

Date _____

☐ Yes, Mike, I have accepted Christ as my personal Saviour and would like to receive my personal gift copy of your book *31 Keys To A New Beginning.* (B 48) #DC10

Name _____

Address _____

City _____ State _____ Zip_____

Phone (   )_____ Birthdate _____

Occupation_____

You are a special person to me, and I believe you are special to God. I want to help you in every way I can. Let me hear from you when you are facing spiritual needs or experiencing a conflict in your life, or if you just want to know that someone really cares. Write me. I will pray for your needs. And I will write you back something that I know will help you receive the miracle you need.

Mike, here are my special needs at this time:
-Please Print-

_____

_____

_____

_____

_____

_____

_____

_____

_____

_____

_____

_____

Mail To:
MIKE MURDOCK
The Wisdom Center • P.O. Box 99 • Dallas, Texas 75221

WILL YOU BECOME A WISDOM KEY PARTNER?

1. TELEVISION - The Way Of The Winner, a nationally-syndicated weekly TV program features Mike Murdock's teaching and music.

2. WTC - Wisdom Training Center where Dr. Murdock trains those preparing for full-time ministry in a special 70 Hour Training Program.

3. MISSIONS - Recent overseas outreaches include crusades to East Africa, Brazil and Poland; 1,000 Young Minister's Handbooks sent to India to train nationals for ministry to their people..

4. MUSIC - Millions of people have been blessed by the anointed songwriting and singing talents of Mike Murdock, who has recorded over 20 highly-acclaimed albums.

5. LITERATURE - Best-selling books, teaching tapes and magazines proclaim the Wisdom of God.

6. CRUSADES - Multitudes are ministered to in crusades and seminars throughout America as Mike Murdock declares life-giving principles from God's Word.

7. SCHOOLS OF WISDOM - Each year Mike Murdock hosts Schools of Wisdom for those who want personalized and advanced training for achieving their dreams and goals.

I want to personally invite you to be a part of this ministry!

WISDOM KEY
PARTNERSHIP PLAN

Dear Partner,

God has brought us together! I love representing you as I spread His Wisdom in the world. Will you become my Faith-Partner? Your Seed is powerful. When you sow, three benefits are guaranteed: PROTECTION *(Mal. 3:10-11),* FAVOR *(Luke 6:38),* FINANCIAL PROSPERITY *(Deut. 8:18). Please note the four levels as a monthly Wisdom Key Faith Partner. Complete the response sheet and rush it to me immediately. Then focus your expectations for the 100-fold return (Mark 10:30)!*

Your Faith Partner,

Mike Murdock

Yes, Mike, I want to be a Wisdom Key Partner with you. Please rush The Wisdom Key Partnership Pak to me today!

☐ **FOUNDATION PARTNER...**Yes, Mike, I want to be a Wisdom Key Foundation Partner. Enclosed is my first monthly Seed-Faith Promise of $15.

☐ **SEED-A-DAY...**Yes, Mike, I want to be a Wisdom Key Partner as a Seed-a-Day member. Enclosed is my first monthly Seed-Faith Promise of $30.

☐ **COVENANT OF BLESSING...**Yes, Mike, I want to be a Wisdom Key Partner as a Covenant of Blessing member. Enclosed is my first Seed-Faith Promise of $58.

☐ **THE SEVENTY...**Yes, Mike, I want to be a Wisdom Key Partner as a member of The Seventy. Enclosed is my first monthly Seed-Faith Promise of $100.

TOTAL ENCLOSED $ _____   #DC10

Name _____

Address _____

City _____State _____Zip_____

Phone ( ) _____Birthday _____

Mail To:

MIKE MURDOCK

The Wisdom Center • P.O. Box 99 • Dallas, Texas 75221

123

WISDOM KEY PARTNERSHIP PAK

When you become a Wisdom Key Monthly Faith Partner or a part of The Seventy, you will receive our Partnership Pak which includes:

1. *Special Music Cassette*
2. *101 Wisdom Keys Book*
3. *Partnership Coupon Book*

Yes Mike! I Want To Be Your Partner!

❏ Enclosed is my best Seed-Faith Gift of $_____.

❏ I want to be a Wisdom Key Partner! Enclosed is my first Seed-Faith gift of $____ for the first month.

❏ Please rush my special Partnership Pak. (#PP02)

Name _____

Address _____

City _____State _____Zip _____

Phone ( )_____

#DC10

Mail To:

MIKE MURDOCK

The Wisdom Center • P.O. Box 99 • Dallas, Texas 75221

4 POWER-PACKED TAPE SERIES BY MIKE MURDOCK

HOW TO WALK THROUGH FIRE

The 4 basic causes of conflict and how to react in a personal crisis, which are extremely helpful for those who are walking through the fires of marriage difficulty, divorce, depression, and financial adversity. (TS5) Six Tape Series

$30

THE ASSIGNMENT

Do you wonder why you are here? What are you to do? These tapes will unlock the hidden treasures inside you to fulfill the *Assignment* God has called you to. 160 Wisdom Keys that can reveal the purpose of God. (TS22) Six Tape Series

$30

WOMEN THAT MEN CANNOT FORGET

Discover the success secrets of two of the most remarkable women in history...and how their secrets can help you achieve your dreams and goals! Both men and women will enjoy these wisdom secrets from the lives of Ruth and Esther. (TS31)Six Tape Series

$30

THE GRASSHOPPER COMPLEX

A must for those who need more self-confidence! It reveals the secrets of overcoming every giant you face in achieving your personal dreams and goals. (TS3)Six Tape Series

$30

**Order All Four Series
& Pay Only $100**

6 Wisdom Books

WISDOM FOR CRISIS TIMES

Discover the Wisdom Keys to dealing with tragedies, stress and times of crisis. Secrets that will unlock the questions in the  right way to react in life situations. (Paperback)

(BK08) 118 Pages.....$7

THE DOUBLE DIAMOND PRINCIPLE

58 Master Secrets For Total Success, in the life of Jesus that will help you achieve your dreams and goals. (Paperback)

(BK71) 118 Pages.....$7

SEEDS OF WISDOM

One-Year Daily Devotional. A 374 page devotional with topics on dreams and goals, relationships, miracles, prosperity and more! (Paperback)

(BK02) 374 Pages.....$10

WISDOM FOR WINNING

The best-selling handbook for achieving success. If you desire to be successful and happy, this is the book for you! (Paperback)

(BK23) 280 Pages.....$9

ONE-YEAR TOPICAL BIBLE

A One-Minute reference Bible. 365 topics; spiritual, topical and easy to read. A collection of Scriptures relating to specific topics that challenge and concern you. (Paperback)

(BK03) 374 Pages.....$10

DREAM SEEDS

What do you dream of doing with you life? What would you attempt to do if you knew it was impossible to fail? This 118-page book helps you answer these questions and much more! (Paperback)

(BK20) 118 Pages.....$7

ORDER FORM

Item No.	Name of Item	Quantity	Price Per Item	Total
#TS22	The Assignment Tapes		30.00	$
#TS5	How To Walk Through Fire Tapes		30.00	$
#TS3	The Grasshopper Complex Tapes		30.00	$
#TS3	Women Men Cannot Forget Tapes		30.00	$
	All 4 Tape Series For $100.00			$
#BK20	Dream Seeds Book		7.00	$
#BK23	Wisdom For Winning Book		9.00	$
#BK20	Seeds of Wisdom Book (374 Pgs)		10.00	$
#BK71	Double Diamond Principle Book		7.00	$
#BK08	Wisdom For Crisis Times Book		7.00	$
#BK03	One Minute Topical Bible (374 Pgs)		10.00	$
SORRY NO C.O.D's		Add 10% For Shipping		$
		(Canada add 20%)		$
		Enclosed is my Seed-Faith Gift for Your Ministry.		$
#DC10		Total Amount Enclosed		$

Please Print

Name

Address

City

State　　　　　　　　　　Zip

Phone(hm)　　　　　　　(wk)

☐ Check　　☐ Money Order　　☐ Cash

☐ Visa　　☐ MasterCard　　☐ AMEX

Signature_____

Card#

Expiration Date _____

☐ Send Free Catalog & Free Subscription To Newsletter *Wisdom Talk*

Mail To:

MIKE MURDOCK

The Wisdom Center • P.O. Box 99 • Dallas, Texas 75221